LANGUAGE THROUGH LIVING

for hearing-impaired children

Morag Clark

HODDER AND STOUGHTON
LONDON   SYDNEY   AUCKLAND   TORONTO

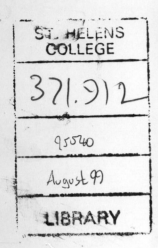
Copyright © 1989 Morag Clark

First published 1989

British Library Cataloguing in Publication Data
Clark, Morag
  Language through living for hearing-impaired
  children.
  1. Deaf children. Education. Communication.
  Techniques
  I. Title
  371.91'23

ISBN 0 340 50537 0

Typeset by Wearside Tradespools, Fulwell, Sunderland.
Printed and bound in Great Britain for
Hodder and Stoughton Educational,
a division of Hodder and Stoughton Ltd,
Mill Road, Dunton Green, Sevenoaks, Kent
by TJ Press Ltd, Padstow.

Contents

About the Author   iv

Acknowledgments   iv

1   Introduction   1

2   The Interactionist Auditory Oral Approach   7

3   The Use of Residual Hearing/Hearing-aids   16

4   Creating a Listening Environment   25

5   Language Through the Daily Routine
    of the Home   37

6   Language Through Other Activities
    with Parents   48

7   Language Through the Pre-school   57

8   Language Through Entry to Primary School   70

9   The Way Ahead   83

References   88

Index   91

About the Author

Coming from the field of ordinary education into work with hearing-impaired children, Morag Clark has a sound basis against which to assess progress. The former Principal of Birkdale School (for hearing-impaired children) she has helped to develop a way of life for these children which not only allows them to attain good educational standards, but which also helps them to develop significant enough competence in spoken language to feel at home in society at large.

Now in her retirement, she is Overseas Adviser to a developing programme for hearing-impaired children at Anadolu University, Eskişehir, Turkey. In addition, she is involved with programmes in Singapore and Tokyo and visits other countries by request. She has also developed a series of four teaching packs (video tapes with written commentaries) in conjunction with MUTV, Manchester University, which are used worldwide in parent and teacher training programmes.

Morag Clark has recently been awarded an MBE for her work in this field.

Acknowledgments

I should like to acknowledge all the help and support I have had from Eileen Tomkinson (Principal of Birkdale School for hearing-impaired children) and the following members of her staff: Barbara Pattison, Sarah Richards, Elizabeth Rothwell and Martin Smith. I am also grateful to professor Yilmaz Büyükerşen (Rector of Anadolu University, Eskişehir, Turkey) and to Umran Tufekçioğlu for their encouragement and support. I should also like to express my thanks to the photographer Kenan Şanlier.

I owe a real debt of gratitude to my sister May Clark and her friend Eva Handley for the genuine interest they have displayed throughout and for their help in checking the manuscript. My final word of thanks must be to all parents and pupils, past and present of the programmes of Birkdale and Eskişehir who provided the experience upon which this book is based.

= 1 =
Introduction

If we are going to persist in our educational enterprise it is urgent that we learn to do it better.

(Donaldson, 1978)

The above words were written in relation to the school experience in general. They have, however, a special significance for those concerned with the education of hearing-impaired children. At no time in history have opportunities for these children been greater, and yet large numbers of them leave school today without fluency of spoken language and with very low levels of educational attainment.

The author has over thirty years' experience in the field of the education of hearing-impaired children and has written this book in the hope that it will lead parents and professionals to a fuller understanding of what it is possible for these children to achieve today. From a sound theoretical basis it deals with practical issues in such a way that it demonstrates how more and more children with severe and profound hearing losses could share the opportunities, already enjoyed by some, that lead to a level of spoken language that is functional for life in society at large.

Over the centuries, and until quite recently, the term 'deaf' has been used to describe those who have a hearing loss. Nowadays, thanks to technological advances, it is possible to establish the extent of the hearing loss and to make use of any residual hearing through the fitting of appropriate hearing-aids. As a result, the term 'hearing impaired' with its emphasis on *hearing*, has now generally replaced that of 'deaf'. It is important to realise that this modern term 'hearing impaired' applies to the whole range of hearing loss and includes those with severe and profound hearing losses as well as those with mild to moderate losses.

The British Society of Audiology (1988), with the endorsement of the British Association of Teachers of the Deaf, have recently published a list of four descriptors of hearing impairment based on the average pure tone hearing loss across the five frequencies 250–4000Hz. This should help to establish a degree of uniformity when hearing losses are under discussion:

Audiometric Descriptor	*dB HL*
Mild hearing loss	20–40
Moderate hearing loss	41–70

| Severe hearing loss | 71–95 |
| Profound hearing loss | in excess of 95 |

Although the degree of hearing loss is by no means the sole basis from which decisions are taken regarding educational placement, it is certainly a significant pointer to the child's probable special educational needs. Many children with mild hearing losses do not require hearing-aids and find conditions in ordinary schools too noisy to use and benefit from them. A favourable position in class and a determined effort to ensure that all staff dealing with the child are aware of his hearing problem often suffice to meet the needs of such a child.

Most children with moderate hearing losses, if fitted with appropriate hearing-aids, can manage well in ordinary classes with support from a specialist teacher of the hearing impaired. Even when the hearing loss comes into the severe or profound category, it is possible for many children to integrate fully into classes of children with normal hearing. Children with severe to profound losses, however, require considerable regular support from a visiting specialist teacher of the hearing impaired. Where this is not available, it may well be in the child's best interest to be placed in a special unit or special school for hearing-impaired children.

The term 'hearing impaired' covers the full range of those who may suffer from a hearing loss, from babies to those whose problems of hearing have come on with old age. Any degree of hearing loss, at any age, may have far reaching effects. Hearing is of such importance to us in our daily lives. It is the sense that brings us so much information about the world around us and the sense through which we develop and maintain the skills to communicate with the people in that world.

The age at which a hearing loss first occurs is very significant. Those who lose their hearing after they have acquired fluent spoken language are in a very different position from those who are born with impaired hearing. This book is concerned with the latter group and with those who lost their hearing before acquiring language. It also concentrates particularly on those whose hearing loss is severe or profound.

There is no doubt that the presence of a significant hearing loss from birth, or from before fluency has developed in the mother tongue, is a major obstacle to the development of easy spoken communication. It is, however, one that can be overcome if parents and professionals work together to surround the young hearing-impaired child with a rich linguistic environment and one in which listening skills can be developed to the full.

All over the world there are young men and women who, in days past would have been 'deaf and dumb' on account of the severity of their hearing losses, but who are in fact able to hold their own in society at large, quite independently. This must be attributed to the fact that they have developed the ability to understand and to make themselves understood in fluent spoken language. There are also, however, large numbers of today's young hearing-impaired adults who have *not* developed such linguistic fluency. An examination of the linguistic environments in which they have grown up would go a long way towards accounting for the very wide differences between the oral competence of the two groups.

There are many approaches to the education of hearing-impaired children. Some incorporate manual systems using a form of finger-spelling or signing, others use cued speech which provides visual cues at the mouth to make lipreading easier. Other approaches use no form of manual support but rely heavily on written back-up to the spoken word from a very young age. All such systems lay emphasis on visual cues from the earliest possible age. This is something that is absent from the experience of a young child with normal hearing at the early language learning stage. Those who are working with hearing-impaired children on an auditory oral approach, that is heavily dependent on good interaction with those in the environ-ment, do not rely on such visual support. They are finding that with the hearing-aids available today, it is possible for hearing-impaired children to learn language in the same way as their hearing counter-parts. Although hearing-impaired children within such an approach combine auditory with visual information, as we all do in a com-munication situation, they become more auditorily aware than those in systems which deliberately provide additional visual cues. It is

Normal language input from teacher while hearing-impaired child's attention is devoted to the task in hand

being found that their whole behaviour has a degree of normality about it and their language has a degree of fluency that can make observers doubt the severity of their hearing losses.

Unfortunately, many professionals working with hearing-impaired children have not experienced the way of life which allows such fluency to develop. As a result, they tend to explain away these orally competent young people as 'exceptions'. An overview of approaches

Figure 1.1   *Distribution of hearing loss*

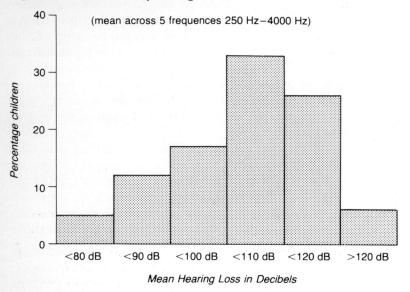

Figure 1.2   *Distribution of WISC performance IQ*

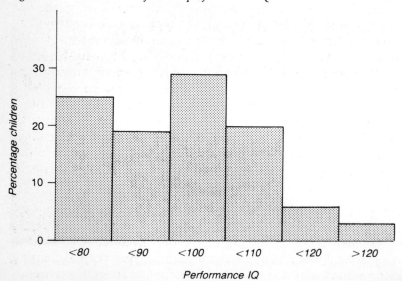

Figure 1.3 *Distribution of social class groups*

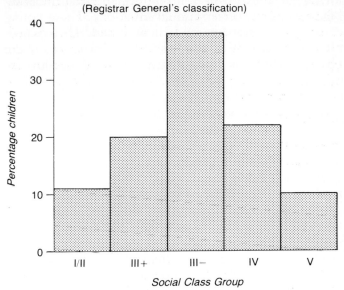

to the education of hearing-impaired children in the USA, reported by Quigley and Kretschmer (1982), indicates that:

> Deaf children in incontestably oral programmes tend to develop better language skills than do deaf children in the general school population.

Quigley and Kretschmer, however, go on to explain that deaf children placed in these programmes are often more select in socio-economic status, IQ and other factors than deaf children in general. The assumption that only hearing-impaired children from specially advantageous backgrounds and with above average intelligence can develop good oral communication skills could not be further from reality. Figures 1.1, 1.2 and 1.3 give a breakdown of the background of 180 children on role at Birkdale School for Hearing-Impaired Children (England, 1984–5) where the author spent twenty-nine years of her professional life. There, hearing-impaired children from all levels of the social scale and from a very wide range of ability, some of whom have significant handicaps in addition to hearing loss, come through to a level of conventional communicative competence that allows them to live their lives independently in a world full of hearing people. Similar young people are to be found in *similar* programmes the world over.

Almost without exception, the thing that orally competent young hearing-impaired people have in common, is that each has learned to use even minimal residual hearing to the full, in an environment in which they have been surrounded by nothing but normal, natural language presented at a normal rate of utterance. In such surroundings they have learned to combine their residual hearing with the visual cues of normal facial expression, lip movements and the body language available to us all in conversational situations. These young hearing-impaired people do not live in a silent world. Their whole behaviour is different from that of the 'visual deaf' who do. If the term 'deaf' is to be applied to this group it must be qualified. They are the 'listening deaf'.

The management of the environment in which hearing-impaired children spend their formative years is all important. This book is written to help parents and professionals to come to a better understanding of the essential features of an environment in which children with severe and profound hearing losses come to develop fluent oral communication skills.

The approach advocated is described in general terms in Chapter Two. Chapters Three and Four examine, from different angles, what is involved in using residual hearing to the full. The importance of the parents' part in a young child's language learning process is the substance of Chapters Five and Six. In Chapters Seven and Eight, educational issues are discussed and followed through from pre-school placement to the beginning of the primary school stage. Chapter Nine looks to the future in the light of the issues that have been examined in the previous chapters.

=== 2 ===
The Interactionist Auditory Oral Way of Life

> *The most effective means of developing spoken language will [also] remain its use in real life communicative situations involving the hearing-impaired child and his teachers, parents and speaking peers.*
>
> (Ling, 1986)

Every word in this somewhat cumbersome chapter heading is important. Together these words summarise the content of the book. Notice, however, that they do not describe a *method* of working with hearing-impaired children, but rather *a way of life* for them.

Oral

Working back along the title it is suggested that this should be an *oral* way of life. When parents are first made aware of the presence of a hearing loss in a young child, one of their early questions is often, 'Will my child learn to talk or will he be deaf and dumb?' The vast majority of hearing-impaired children have parents who have normal hearing and whose natural means of communication is spoken language. There are those, associated with the deaf community, who claim that sign language is the 'natural' language of any deaf child. It must be made clear that this cannot be so for children born into the homes of parents with normal hearing, who will at all times surround their child with normal spoken language. The argument holds only for the very small minority of hearing-impaired children whose parents are signing deaf adults. Lynas, Huntington, and Tucker (1988) estimate that:

> Only 3 per cent of severely and profoundly deaf children (that is children with hearing losses greater than 70dB) have both parents who are deaf and a further 7 per cent have one parent who is deaf.

It must be borne in mind too that an increasingly large number of today's young hearing-impaired parents have themselves developed fluent communication skills and are able to surround their children with spoken language.

In addition, it should be realised that some hearing-impaired parents, themselves dependent on sign language for their main means of communication, are well aware of the limitations that this has placed on their lives. They are anxious that their children should have every opportunity to develop the fluent spoken language that they have seen in many of today's young orally competent hearing-impaired adults.

Prior to the identification of a hearing loss in a child, the development of spoken language is something that is taken for granted. Although it is seldom even mentioned, because it seems to happen so naturally, there is undoubtedly an underlying awareness of its importance to us as human beings. Meers (1976) states:

> Learning to understand what someone else says and to express oneself
> in spoken language are stages of a process peculiar to human beings.

Once a hearing loss has been diagnosed in a young child, it is often the fear that this process will be denied their young child that alarms parents more than anything else. They must have early assurance that this need not be the case, if the linguistic environment in which the child grows up is managed appropriately.

As the pages of this book unfold, a description of good practice, based on sound theory, will offer guidelines to parents and professionals seeking to provide adequate opportunities for hearing-impaired children to develop fluent spoken language. Much of the advice will be simple and may not seem *special* enough to those seeking to help children who seem to have such very special needs. A great deal of it will consist of attention to detail in relation to hearing-aids. The rest will be concerned, not so much with doing something *different* as with doing *more of normality*.

Unfortunately, in the past, various so-called oral approaches have had, at best, only limited degrees of success. Many of today's adult deaf community were educated in schools that claimed to use the oral method, and yet they are more at home expressing themselves in sign language. It must be realised that there are many varieties of oralism. In traditional schools for the deaf the oral approach adopted was often rigid and restrictive. Within such a setting children were offered teacher-selected vocabulary and set sentence patterns which did little to meet their true linguistic needs. In addition, they often had daily sessions of analytical speech teaching which isolated speech from language. In most cases this type of oralism had been superimposed on a manual system that had previously been in existence in the schools. In such a setting the children continued to use sign language in all out-of-class situations. Kretschmer and Kretschmer (1978) highlight this difficulty. When discussing the sampling of children used in many of the comparative studies in the USA they point out:

> A difficulty with comparative studies on communication modes is that

many purport to use children exposed to certain communication modes when, in fact, these modes are, at best, only employed in the classroom.

The Kretschmers go on to describe how investigators have drawn their 'orally educated' sample from settings where manual communication was the mode used in all but classroom situations. They make the point that such practice is not acceptable to today's educators using a truly oral approach.

The situation is further complicated by the fact that some of the present day adult deaf were educated in environments within which they did not have access to finger-spelling or signing, but within which their *eyes* were looked upon as *substitutes* for their *ears*. Vocabulary was often specially selected for them because it was easy to lipread and language was *taught* in a way that is quite different from that in which a child with normal hearing *develops* fluency in his mother tongue. The author found herself in such a situation in the first programme for hearing-impaired children in which she taught. A rigid language scheme was followed class by class. At the early stages lists of nouns and lists of the imperative forms of certain verbs had to be memorised by the children, for example:

nouns – window, door, table, chair, wall
verbs – hop, walk, skip, run, jump

Sentences were then built combining these words and were recited by the class as a whole, for example:

Walk to the window.
Jump to the door.

It is little wonder that such sterile language was rejected by the children and that they built up a system of signs and gestures in which to express what they really wanted to say in out-of-class situations.

Within such an approach the method of presenting language, too, was abnormal. Objects were held up to the lips to draw attention to the lipread pattern. In many situations there was an early and heavy reliance on the written word. Such practices die hard and remnants of them are to be found in many programmes for hearing-impaired children today. Although nowadays the children within such environments wear hearing-aids, any help that the aids give them tends to be looked upon as a bonus to what the eye can supply.

Pollack (1970) who was one of the pioneers in helping children with severe and profound hearing losses to use residual hearing to the full, points out the danger of substituting eyes for ears:

There can be no compromise. Once emphasis is placed on looking there will be divided attention and the unimpaired modality – vision – will be victorious.

With the hearing-aids that are available today it is possible for residual hearing to be harnessed in such a way that the development of fluent oral language in a natural way becomes a realistic possibility, even for those with severe and profound hearing losses.

Auditory

The next word in the chapter heading suggests that this is to be an *auditory* way of life. In such an approach, emphasis is not placed on visual cues through directing the child to watch the lips, attend to cued speech, finger-spelling, signing or to the written word. Instead, attention is turned to the development of an awareness of sound. At the same time it must be clearly understood that lipreading is not denied the child and that all the visual cues available in normal communication situations are there. People with normal hearing depend quite heavily on facial expression or on body language as they seek to share meaning in everyday conversation. It seems abnormal to deny such natural visual cues to a child whose auditory cues are reduced on account of a severe or profound hearing loss.

Advances in hearing-aid technology have greatly improved opportunities for hearing-impaired children. Stone and Adam (1986) testify to this:

> Due to technological advances in the past twenty years, it is possible to provide meaningful and important speech information even to most profoundly hearing-impaired children.

Hearing-aids can now reach more children than ever before and, in almost every case, even children with profound hearing losses can be brought out of a world of silence into a world of sound.

Transistorised personal hearing-aids have been freely available in Britain since the late 1950s. It is exciting to meet large numbers of young adults with severe and profound hearing losses who are able to take their places effectively within the normal life of their neighbourhood, not as 'the deaf' – a sub-culture of society – but as people in the normal community who have learned how to cope with a hearing loss. At the same time it should be understood that, while coping, these young people do experience some difficulties that may never go away, for example, problems with conversation when in a group. Those with profound hearing losses may also have speech which is not always understood on first hearing and they have to learn how to cope with this situation.

In some ways those hearing-impaired young adults who have, as Huizing (1960) said, 'learned to integrate hearing into their personalities', highlight the plight of those who have not had the opportunity to do so. Where voices have the old 'deaf' sound and where oral fluency has not developed, almost without fail, an investigation will show that the key to the difference between these two groups of young people with similar hearing losses lies, not in innate differences within the young people themselves, but rather in the type of auditory linguistic environment in which they spent their formative years. There are so many possible reasons for this. The young people with poor levels of oral communication may not have had appropriate hearing-aids or there may well have been features of the environment in which they grew up that reduced the benefit of the hearing-aids. At any one time in Birkdale School there were always a few children who had very 'deaf' voices and mannerisms, and whose communicative behaviour marked them out as different from the general population of severely and profoundly hearing-impaired children in the school. Each of these had come into the programme after the age of six from a programme of a very different nature. At one time it was possible to find a matched pair for each of eight children in this group. The children were matched for degree of hearing loss, IQ, social class group, age of diagnosis of hearing loss, and age on issue of hearing-aid. In every case the only feasible explanation for the vastly different quality of spoken language lay in the lack of ability of the late entrants to use their residual hearing to the full. Each had come from a different programme, but from one that had trained them to rely mainly on vision in communication situations.

Another interesting by-product of the comparison of the two groups was that their general conversational behaviour was very different. The late entrants did not seem to know the rules of conversation which are learned unconsciously through regular interaction with those in the environment. It could be that there was not enough meaningful interaction in their previous environments to stimulate them to make sense of the minimal auditory cues that reached them.

Interactionist

This way of life involves good *interaction* between hearing-impaired children and those around them. Ling and Ling (1978) make this point clearly:

> It is through the child's search for meaning – through his struggle to determine the speaker's intent – that he comes to realise what acoustic cues are significant.

Today's hearing-aids provide better opportunities than ever before for hearing-impaired children to learn language in the same way as, although more slowly than, their hearing counterparts. The hearing-aids, however, must be used in an environment in which the children are motivated to communicate with those around them and within which there are adults who are good listeners and who are anxious to share meaning with the children. The provision of such an environment is very important for any young child at the language learning stage, whether that child has normal hearing or not. Tough (1977) calls it a 'language enabling' environment and describes it as a situation that encompasses activities which motivate the child to communicate and in which dialogue can play a major role in the fostering and developing of language.

Recent research into early language development places a new importance on the significant adults in the child's environment. Bruner (1983) emphasises the need for the adult to enter with the child 'into a transactional format'. Wells (1981) suggests that:

> The most important basis and motivation for the child's way in to language is to be found in communicating with others.

In the case of those in contact with hearing-impaired children, the responsibility of the adults in the environment is even greater. If these children are to be brought to a level of communicative competence that will allow them to function as independent citizens in society at large, more time must be allowed at the early language learning stage to enable them to interact on a one-to-one basis with those around them. In addition, those adults with whom the children do interact

Child motivated to communicate and to make sense of auditory cues in a shared activity

must be sensitive to the intentions of the children as they seek to express themselves, and parents, in particular, need constructive help in this area. Not only do they need to know how, when and whether to intervene, but they also need to know what to expect at the various stages along the way.

Expectations of the interactionist auditory oral way of life

It is only natural that right from the start, many parents want to know if the way in which they are embarking will allow their child to develop a fluency of spoken language that will make it possible to mix freely and independently in society. In other words, *expectations* must be set for parents. The responsibility for setting those expectations falls on the shoulders of the professionals involved at the time of diagnosis. This is a difficult area. Professionals themselves have their own expectations set in the light of their own experience and this experience differs greatly from one professional to another.

Educational provision for hearing-impaired children differs from one geographical area to another resulting in wide differences in the linguistic capabilities of the young people leaving the various systems. It is obvious that this must affect the expectations of any professionals whose experience is limited to one particular system. The advice given to some parents of newly diagnosed hearing-impaired children is a sad reflection that certain professionals have not themselves been in contact with many of today's severely and profoundly hearing-impaired young people who have developed very competent spoken language. As a result they have not raised their own expectations in the light of the significant progress in the field and are really in no position to give up-to-date advice. In the space of one week, quite recently, the author met three families, each with a hearing-impaired child under the age of eighteen months. There was no doubt that each child seemed to have a very severe or profound hearing loss. At that young age, however, it is impossible to predict just how much useful hearing is present or how well a child will learn to listen. Differences in the expectations of professionals was certainly reflected in the advice offered to these three families. One had been encouraged to do everything possible to ensure that the child's hearing was stimulated to the full, and they understood something of the importance of surrounding the child with meaningful language. On the other hand, both of the other families had been given hearing-aids for their children, but had been told that the aids would be of little use because of the severity of the hearing loss. They had been advised to learn sign language straight away in order to be able to communicate with their children.

The really efficient use of hearing-aids has, to date, been relatively rare and so it is understandable that many still underestimate the value of the aids in the language learning process of hearing-impaired children. It is alarming, however, to find professionals whose experience is so grounded in traditional standards that they offer advice on the basis of the belief expressed by Mindel and Vernon (1974) that 'Continuous efforts to expose the child to sound are an exercise in futility.'

So many questions need to be asked when a hearing-impaired child does not appear to use residual hearing to the full. Where eyes have been trained to take over from ears it may well seem futile to attempt to develop listening skills. That is but one area that needs exploration before statements are made to parents.

When professionals have had the opportunity of meeting hearing-impaired children who have learned to listen and to make amazing use of minimal auditory cues, the picture painted for parents is a very different one. While enthusiasm is being engendered about the possibilities for the long-term, however, parents need to be cautioned that results may not come immediately. They need to be prepared for the fact that there may well be a period in which little *seems* to be happening. Brackett and Pollack (1986) express this well:

> Many children with severe and profound hearing losses may appear totally unresponsive to sound when first seen. An estimate of listening potential must be made after the child has had a fair chance at learning to listen. For children with profound hearing losses several months of wearing amplification and encouraging the child to listen may be required.

In 1986 the author had the mother of profoundly hearing-impaired twins video-taped while she was chatting to the school audiologist about her memories of their early use of hearing-aids (Clark, 1986b). When asked if she saw a real change in their behaviour after the issue of their hearing-aids she replied, 'Well, it was all so gradual really.' To hear such evidence from an experienced mother is very reassuring to parents of children whose hearing losses have recently been diagnosed and who may not be seeing immediate results from the use of hearing-aids.

It is obvious that parents, influenced by professionals well-experienced in the use and value of residual hearing, will have very different expectations from parents influenced by those whose expectations stem from their experience in traditional backgrounds.

However, expectations need not, and indeed should not, be based on the experience of one professional alone. Parents may form their own judgements as they are exposed to available evidence. They need to meet groups of hearing-impaired young people who have been brought up in different educational systems. Herein lies a considerable difficulty. It is relatively easy to find those who spend the majority of their social life in adult deaf communities, but not at all easy to identify the increasingly large number whose ease and fluency of spoken language make it possible for them to be wholly integrated into their local communities. And yet, it is of the utmost importance that the parents of today's hearing-impaired children should have contact with this very group of young hearing-impaired adults, so that they can gain an understanding of the degree of fluency that is possible today for those hearing-impaired children who have enjoyed a truly auditory oral way of life heavily dependent upon the quality of interaction within it.

In an attempt to bring such evidence to parents and professionals who find it difficult to meet orally competent young hearing-impaired adults in their own areas, the author (Clark, 1985, 1986a and 1986b) has produced a series of teaching packs (video-tapes with written commentaries). The material shows a representative sample of young adults with severe and profound hearing losses. Some were diagnosed early and benefited from good parent guidance. Others had their hearing losses diagnosed very late – one girl at the age of five years eight months. Most were the only hearing-impaired child in the family, but some had hearing-impaired brothers and sisters. Three had hearing-impaired parents whose natural means of communication in the home was that of finger-spelling and signing. Several have had to cope, not only with a significant hearing loss, but also with additional handicaps.

As parents, or the professional working with them, are able to view such a cross-section of young hearing-impaired people they often identify some of the problems facing their newly diagnosed child, and at the same time they are often motivated by the obvious ease of communication that these young people have developed. Seeing and/or speaking with hearing-impaired young people with fluent oral communication skills is more powerful in setting expectations than any amount of counselling from a professional. The experience also ensures that truly realistic expectations are set. Parents come to realise that although the speech is fluent and intelligible, in many cases it is not completely normal. They may also be aware of a few grammatical errors and sometimes comment on these. What they do come away with, however, is the certainty that these young people, with hearing losses similar to that of their own child, are wholly at home in the company of hearing people, and that they are able to work and to enjoy life to the full in their local neighbourhoods.

3

The Use of
Residual Hearing/Hearing-aids

> *Hearing-aids are the most important tool available to hearing-impaired children.*
>
> (Ling and Ling, 1978)

No attempt will be made in this chapter to describe procedures for the diagnosis of hearing loss in young children, the fitting of appropriate hearing-aids, or the making of satisfactory earmoulds. Such procedures are well-documented elsewhere (Tucker and Nolan, 1984). The aim of this chapter is to highlight the need for a sense of urgency in these areas and in that of hearing-aid maintenance.

The British National Health Service allows for the free fitting and maintenance of hearing-aids for all who require them. As a result, it is often mistakenly taken for granted that every hearing-impaired child in Britain is adequately 'aided' and will thus have the opportunity to use residual hearing to the full. The author's experience, over a period of twenty-nine years in Birkdale School for Hearing-Impaired Children (serving over twenty local education authorities in the north west of England), proves this to be far from the case. Reed (1984) in his description of the difficulties of maintenance generally, lends weight to the argument that the north west area is not atypical in this respect. Parents and professionals must direct their attention to certain specific aspects of the service if improvements are to come about that will ensure better opportunities for the use of residual hearing of today's hearing-impaired children.

The importance of early diagnosis

Children with normal hearing develop language in the process of living while they interact with those who use the mother tongue. Very soon after birth babies with normal hearing give indications that they are aware of sound, and careful observers may note that different sounds evoke different responses. Before they understand speech, babies derive meaning from voice patterns. All this experience lays the foundations for later development of spoken language.

Thanks to improved hearing-aid technology there are now better opportunities than ever before for hearing-impaired children to develop fluency in their mother tongue, in the same way as their hearing counterparts. Before advantage can be taken of the wide range of hearing-aids now available, the hearing loss must be diagnosed as accurately and as early as possible. Although an increasing number of children *do* have their hearing losses diagnosed early, there are still far too many who do not. It is disappointing that, in spite of the pioneering work of the Ewings (1954), Fry and Whetnall (1954) and others, progress across the years has been so slow.

In 1986 the group of children (85 per cent with mean hearing loss over 90dB) attending Birkdale School, showed the following range of age on diagnosis of hearing loss:

Figure 3.1   *Age at which deafness was diagnosed in children aged between 5.0 and 16.10 years*

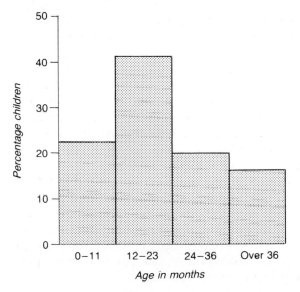

When the figures for the younger group were extracted the picture was brighter, but still leaves no room for complacency (see Figure 3.2).

This problem cannot be attributed to particularly poor services in one geographical area. A survey carried out by Martin *et al.* (1981) for the European Community revealed that less than 50 per cent of children with significant hearing losses had these identified by their third birthday. Davies (1981) reports similar figures for a small study carried out in the London area, but she makes the point that on the whole, the more severe the hearing loss the earlier the diagnosis. This picture must change if the effect of the sensory handicap caused by hearing impairment is to be reduced. The earlier the hearing impair-

Figure 3.2 *Age at which deafness was diagnosed in children aged between 5.0 and 7.10 years*

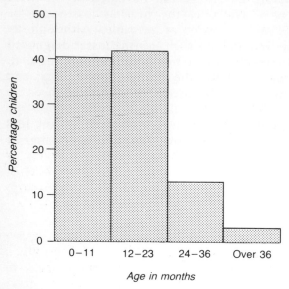

ment is diagnosed the sooner steps can be taken to ensure that any residual hearing can be used to the full. Too much emphasis cannot be put on the importance of bringing the very young hearing-impaired child out of a world of silence into a world of sound at the earliest opportunity. It is vital to take advantage of the time of life when children develop language so naturally and so quickly.

There are, however, for one reason or another, always likely to be some children whose hearing losses are diagnosed late. In some areas there is a disturbing tendency for the parents of these children to be advised to place them in programmes using some form of manual support, on account of the children's late start. It is important to realise that such children can benefit from a wholly auditory oral programme and can develop fluent spoken language within it, although the quality of their voices might never be as good as it would have been had they begun such a programme earlier.

Early fitting of appropriate hearing-aids

Almost every hearing-impaired child has some usable hearing. The author, in the course of over thirty years' work in this field, has encountered only five children who after consistent use of appropriate hearing-aids over a period of many months, continued to show no response to sound. It is interesting to note that all five children were adventitiously deafened – four by meningitis and one by a severe head injury. Three of these children claimed that communication was easier when wearing hearing-aids. Pollack (1970) feels that 'All deaf children should be given the opportunity to use amplification even if no overt responses to sound are observed.' Other professionals, Ling and Ling (1978) and Paterson (1982), also report from long experience, that they have found the majority of hearing-impaired children to have hearing that is useful for language comprehension, if given suitable amplification.

Once a hearing loss has been confirmed, therefore, the early fitting of hearing-aids becomes a priority because it reduces the time that children spend in a world of silence and it provides access to the language that surrounds them daily. If the hearing loss is severe or profound, a child may take a considerable time to become aware of sound and to learn to interpret it. This is an ability that develops gradually if children are adequately 'aided' in a motivating environment.

A wider range of hearing-aids is available at present than at any time in the past. Many of these have an audio input facility which allows for their use with a radio system, thus reducing the problem of distance from microphone. Nolan and Tucker (1981) give a good description of a variety of radio systems and suggestions for their use. A wider choice brings with it a greater weight of responsibility for those working in the area of the selection and fitting of appropriate hearing-aids. Unfortunately, today, too many children are wearing hearing aids that do not meet their audiological needs.

Ensuring that a child has the best possible amplification is a time-consuming process. The audiologist must be aware of, and have access to, a wide range of hearing-aids. Their special characteristics must be known so that it is possible to consider those most likely to meet the child's specific audiological needs. According to the age of the child, an appropriate test must be administered (warble tone or speech) so that comparisons may be made between one model of hearing-aid and another. Where test results are inclusive and there is an element of doubt, a system needs to operate that allows for realistic trial periods with several models. At such a time information about the child's performance when wearing the particular aids under review should be gathered, not only under test conditions in a clinic situation, but also from those who interact with the child regularly in the classroom (if the child is of school age) and, of course, from the parents who should be asked for their observations of the child's reactions to sounds when wearing the hearing-aids in the familiar situation of the home.

Until steps are taken to ensure that attention to detail is observed in the fitting of each child's hearing-aids, it cannot be claimed that hearing-impaired children are having the opportunity to enjoy a truly auditory oral way of life. Much of the severe language delay and many of the poor quality voices to be found among hearing-impaired children undoubtedly have their roots in lack of appropriate amplification in the early years. Stone and Adam (1986) use strong words and go beyond asking for hearing-impaired children to have the opportunity to use residual hearing when they claim. 'Every child has the right to receive and use as much sound, both spoken and environmental, as possible.'

Those who have seen the use that children *can* make, of even minimal amounts of residual hearing, when properly 'aided', are aware that the efficient use of hearing-aids, throughout their waking hours, can revolutionise the lives of today's hearing-impaired children. Testimony to this fact can be found in a paper, given orally, by Huntington (1987) who claimed:

> Technological aids have personally delivered unmeasurable benefits, educationally, socially and professionally. For example, without my hearing-aids I would have found the struggle to complete my secondary education amidst my hearing peers too much to bear.

A young maintenance worker in a hotel speaks from a different background – that of a special school education – when he declares in a video-taped interview 'I can't live without my hearing-aids. I feel I'm lost. I can't hear anything.' (Clark, 1986). His hearing loss is very severe (95dB across the speech range) but his hearing-aids are his lifeline. He is typical of many of today's 'listening' hearing-impaired adults who have had the benefit of appropriate hearing-aids from a young age, and so have enjoyed a truly auditory oral way of life.

Earmoulds

Part of the process of fitting the best possible hearing-aid involves the making of well-fitting earmoulds. This is an area which still gives so much cause for concern that it must be singled out for special attention. It must be realised that the efficient performance of a hearing-aid is very dependent upon the fit of the earmould. In many places there are still great difficulties in ensuring that a consistent supply of comfortable, well-fitting earmoulds is always available.

Not only is it important to attend to the fit of the earmould. Care must be taken to ensure that the material selected for the making of the earmould is appropriate to the child's needs. It is being found in some places that children with severe and profound hearing losses benefit from earmoulds that have been made from all soft material (Dawson, 1977 and Nolan, 1982).

A record was kept of all children who paid first visits to Birkdale School during the two-year period 1982–84. There were forty-eight children in the group. In the local area from which they came, each

Figure 3.3 *State of 96 earmoulds (48 visiting children 1982–84)*

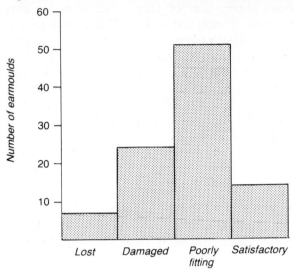

had already been fitted with two hearing-aids (or with one hearing-aid with a y-lead which allows the use of both ears). A total of ninety-six earmoulds was therefore involved. Figure 3.3 gives a summary of the state of these earmoulds.

Notes on Figure 3.3

Lost earmoulds
Of the seven earmoulds lost, six had been missing for a period of more than two weeks. In each case the child was wearing only one of two available hearing-aids.

Damaged or rough earmoulds
Twenty-four earmoulds fell into this category. Of these, eighteen had broken tips and the other six had rough patches on the surface. Parents of four of the children reported the reluctance of their child to wear the earmould in question, although there had been no reluctance on the part of the child with the previous earmould. As a result, one child was wearing no hearing-aid at all because both of the earmoulds were rough, and three other children were wearing only one of their two available hearing-aids. Nine of the parents in this group stated that they had made more than one approach to the responsible professional regarding the state of the earmoulds and in seven cases impressions had been taken for new earmoulds. At the same time, there were reports of long delays in the delivery of new earmoulds after the impressions had been taken and sent away to be processed. All but one child had already waited for at least two weeks.

Earmoulds restricting the output of the hearing-aid

The area of greatest concern was that of poorly fitting earmoulds which caused the parents, and in some cases the children themselves, to turn down the volume of the hearing-aid to stop the feedback which made an unpleasant whistle. Fifty-one earmoulds were limiting the amount of amplification that the child could receive. Perhaps the most worrying feature of this situation was that many of the parents thought that they had solved the problem when they had managed to stop the feedback by turning down the volume of the hearing-aid. They seemed unaware that by so doing they were greatly detracting from the value of the hearing-aid to the child.

Satisfactory earmoulds

Of the fourteen earmoulds that were satisfactory, twelve were worn by six children. The fact that only 6.25 per cent of this random group of hearing-impaired children, from a wide area of the north west of England, were enjoying full benefit from their hearing-aids, on account of the state of the earmoulds, serves to show something of the size of the problem. Until important details of this nature receive attention, it cannot be claimed that hearing-impaired children *even have a chance* to enjoy an auditory oral way of life.

The efficient maintenance of hearing-aids

One of the most neglected areas of all is that of hearing-aid maintenance. If hearing-impaired children are to learn to use residual hearing effectively, they must have a consistent pattern of amplification. This means that the hearing-aids must be working efficiently all the time. Maintenance is a problem worldwide. Stone and Adam (1986) quote two American studies which make depressing reading. Bess (1977), working for the United States Bureau for the Handicapped found that:

> A large proportion of children's hearing-aids in the public school setting do not provide adequate performance.

A more recent study by Osberger (1985) reported that 30–40 per cent of hearing-aids in use with children over the age of seven years six months were non-functional as were 'the majority' of those used by children below that age.

So much is involved in ensuring that hearing-aids are functioning efficiently. Attention must be paid to every detail, every day and this must be a shared responsibility. A system must operate which allows parents, professionals and, in time, the children themselves, to do a subjective daily check on each hearing-aid. In addition, at least once a month, each aid should go through a hearing-aid test box which will

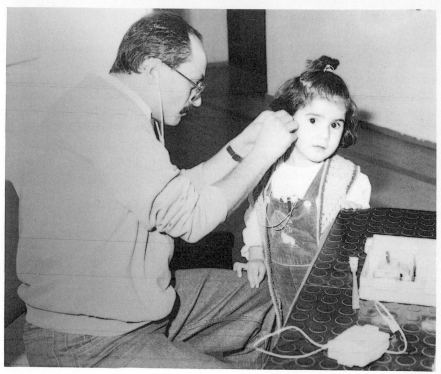

Testing the fit of an earmould in a regular morning hearing-aid check

check its performance against the manufacturer's specification for that particular model.

Once faults are detected, there needs to be a procedure to follow that is known to parents and professionals working with the children. This should provide for on-the-spot repair, or for the availability, at all times, of a replacement hearing-aid of the same type. This whole area is illustrated and dealt with in more detail on a video-tape (Clark, 1986b), but it is of such importance that it must also be raised briefly in this text.

Those involved in the daily routine checking of hearing-aids become very proficient at detecting and diagnosing faults. The task may seem humdrum, but it is one of the most vital parts of any system that seeks to maximise the use of residual hearing. Stethoclips are available and should be standard equipment for those carrying out the hearing-aid check. Their use allows the complete hearing-aid system to be tested and the quality of the signal to be monitored. During the daily check attention should be paid to the state of the battery, the lead, the receiver, the microphone and the earmould.

Checking the auditory pathway

A simple factor that is all too often neglected is the state of the child's ear. It is important to check that the ear canal is clear. This is not a lengthy procedure and a quick weekly examination of the ear canal ensures that any build-up of excessive wax is detected. This is very important because a build-up of wax can cause an additional barrier which impedes the passage of sound and, in some cases, can reflect the amplified signal to contribute to acoustic feedback. In addition, the presence of wax presents problems when the time comes for a new earmould impression to be taken.

The condition of the middle ear, too, should be monitored regularly. Problems of middle ear fluid and Eustachian tube dysfunction are common and can be detected by the regular use of an automatic tympanometer as a screening procedure. This gives an indication of the compliance of the middle ear and the pressure within the middle ear cavity. If a problem is detected early, referral for a full diagnostic test can reduce the chance of a persistent extra conductive element which might add to an already significant sensori neural hearing loss.

Regular hearing-aid review procedures

A hearing-aid, once fitted, is not necessarily the hearing-aid for life. The needs of hearing-aid wearers change as their educational and social environments change. In addition, new hearing-aids with new features come on to the market. Any service seeking to give optimum opportunities to hearing-impaired children must, therefore, have built into it a regular review procedure. This must allow for the children's performance on their present hearing-aids to be established and to be compared with that on newer or more advanced models, and for a change to be prescribed when found necessary.

Conclusion

There is nothing glamorous about the work outlined in this chapter. It is, however, no optional extra but, rather, the very foundation on which an efficient auditory oral way of life for hearing-impaired children can be built. It must be realised that when all six areas dealt with in this chapter operate efficiently, the stage will only just have been reached when it can be claimed that hearing-impaired children are being managed auditorily in such a way that they have the possibility of learning to use their residual hearing to the full.

= 4 =
Creating a Listening Environment

> *Suitable amplification may be the corner-stone of auditory rehabilitation, but it is only the beginning.*
>
> (Bamford and Saunders, 1985)

Attitudes to the use of residual hearing

The greatest single factor in the creation of an environment in which a young hearing-impaired child (fitted with appropriate hearing-aids) learns to listen, is that of attitude.

The attitude of the professionals offering guidance

When parents have a child diagnosed as hearing-impaired they are often bewildered, but almost always they are also anxious to 'do something' as soon as possible. This provides the professional offering guidance to the family, with a wonderful opportunity to involve them in the very practical task of hearing-aid management.

The effectiveness of the advice offered to the parents depends on the attitude of the professional at this crucial stage in the life of the young hearing-impaired child. A great deal of excellent advice is given, but there are still too many instances of valuable opportunities for the early use of residual hearing being wasted because a professional is insufficiently convinced of the *absolute necessity* of auditory stimulation through the best possible hearing-aids from the earliest possible age. Few admit to complacency in this area but, in reality, the drive needed to ensure that all the details of hearing-aid issue and management are attended to, is exhibited only by those who see this as a real priority in relation to the child's future development of spoken language.

It was all too obvious to the author, when dealing with over thirty professionals engaged in pre-school guidance work with families of hearing-impaired children all over north-west England, that attitudes varied greatly in this vital sphere of the work. A few examples of the variety of responses made by professionals to the question 'How has the child accepted the hearing-aids?' illustrates this point well. These may be divided into two categories:

(*a*) Passive acceptance of the problem.
(*b*) Active involvement in the solution of the problem.

Passive acceptance of the problem

- 'He doesn't like his hearing-aids but he's so very young, you see. He'll grow into them perhaps.'
- 'I don't think he gets anything from his hearing-aids and that's why he won't wear them.'
- 'Well they're great big bulky things for such a little one to wear. I can understand that she doesn't want them.'
- 'They whistle all the time. It drives her mother mad. I couldn't stand it myself.'

Each of these responses came from a different professional, as did each of those listed next.

Active involvement in the solution of the problem

- 'It's been difficult to get her to accept the hearing-aids but we've all persevered and now they go on with her clothes in the morning and come off when she goes to bed at night.'
- 'Moulds are a problem with such a little one, and we're not very popular at the local earmould clinic because we keep asking for some that fit better. Never mind, we're winning, and he's certainly hearing sound through those aids.'
- 'I think that there must be a tolerance problem. She's been so difficult to fit with hearing-aids. She was really unhappy with the first two sets that we tried, but the ones that she's wearing now have good compression and she seems very happy with them.'
- 'I'm not getting much support from the parents yet, but I'm making extra visits at the moment and I was so pleased to find the hearing-aids on when I dropped in unexpectedly the other day.'

Such contrasting attitudes speak volumes. There is no doubt that parents can detect whether or not a professional is merely paying lip-service to the possible value of a hearing-aid to the child, or whether there is full commitment to, and enthusiasm for, the stimulation of any residual hearing that remains, through the regular use of two appropriate, well-fitting hearing-aids.

It is therefore, very important for those guiding parents to keep abreast of the developments in hearing-aid technology. It is also important that they should take positive steps to acquaint themselves with some of today's 'listening' hearing-impaired young adults who serve as such an encouragement to any who may be inclined to give up when initial progress is slow.

Positive attitudes on the part of professionals involved with the families of hearing-impaired children around the time of diagnosis, and through the early years, lay the foundations of a good listening environment for the hearing-impaired child.

The attitude of parents

It is a fact of life that young hearing-aid users rely heavily on their parents to ensure that their aids are used to their full potential.

(Nolan and Tucker, 1981)

While it is very important for parents to be able to call on, and to expect help from professionals, it must never be forgotten that the primary responsibility for the child rests with the parents. In no area is this responsibility greater than in that of efficient hearing-aid management.

Hearing-aids are not very attractive and this may well be a reason for their being less socially acceptable than spectacles. As a result, some parents are reluctant to insist on their regular use by their child. If, however, parents can be led to understand the important part that these hearing-aids can play in their child's language development, they become motivated to act and they develop positive attitudes towards the aids. Professionals have a responsibility to ensure that parents are well enough informed to understand both the advantages and the limitations of hearing-aids in their child's case. A fine balance must be kept between under-informing parents and overloading them with too many technical details.

In some cases it is possible to demonstrate early on that the child responds to voice when wearing the hearing-aids, but makes no response to the same level of voice, or to a louder voice without the aids. In cases like this there is usually no problem in helping parents to understand the advantage of, and the necessity for the regular use of the hearing-aids.

In other cases, however, in the early days after the fitting of the hearing-aids there may be very little difference in the child's behaviour with or without the aids. Parents, in such circumstances, need a great deal of support and reassurance that a child with a very severe hearing loss may take time to *learn* to listen. It often proves helpful at a time like this to introduce parents to the parents of an older child who was slow to show response to sound after the issue of hearing-aids, but who is now obviously benefiting from their use.

The regular daily use of hearing-aids may bring with it many problems related to maintenance. It is understandable that if parents see no difference in the behaviour of their child due to the use of the hearing-aids, they may well feel disinclined to persevere. It is so important that the relationship between the professional offering guidance and the parents is such that the parents feel free to express their true feelings about their child's use of hearing-aids, and that they do not cover up their difficulties by giving polite responses which they know will satisfy the professional, when questions are asked about the regular use of the hearing-aids. Once parents look on the hearing-aids positively and ensure that they are used from rising until going to bed, the foundations of a listening environment have been strengthened.

The attitude of the child

Some hearing-impaired children accept their hearing-aids instantly and show pleasure in their use. Others, at the early stages, tolerate them and show neither pleasure nor displeasure. Some react to their use by becoming quiet. This often causes anxiety in the parents, and it must be explained to them that the child is experiencing sound for the first time and has become quiet in order to listen to it.

The children who present real problems are those who actively dislike their hearing-aids and who keep trying to remove them. Parents, aware of the value of the hearing-aids to the child, are often very distressed when this happens. They feel guilty that they cannot make the child wear the aids. At such a time they need regular help and support. Above all, they need reassurance that their child is not an isolated case and, if at all possible they should be introduced to the parents of an older child, now well-adjusted to the wearing of hearing-aids, who was slow to accept them initially. Professionals must share the anxiety of the parents of children who have difficulty in accepting hearing-aids and must work along with them, devising ways of distracting the child's attention after the earmoulds have been put in, or put back in! The quiet confidence with which earmoulds are replaced transmits to the child the idea that, as one parent put it, 'These are there to stay'. Sometimes a child is helped to accept hearing-aids by seeing other children wearing them too. However it is done, parents and professional must work together to ensure that the child comes to use the hearing-aids from morning until night as part of the process of living and, as time goes on, to detect and report when the aids are not working efficiently.

Learning to listen

In a truly auditory oral approach attention is not focused on the *degree of deafness*, but on *the potential hearing* that the children have, once they have been fitted with appropriate hearing-aids which they wear all their waking hours. Parents are encouraged to think in terms of day-long auditory experience, not in those of specific sessions of auditory training. Pollack (1970) makes this clear when she says:

> Sessions of acoustic exercises are not the answer to the child's need. Listening must be a continuous activity.

So often, in the early stages, just after diagnosis, parents feel inadequate. Vaughan (1981), herself the parent of a hearing-impaired child, describes the anxiety of a parent trying to come to terms with the implications of a child's hearing loss in relation to possible potential listening ability. She says that a question which is uppermost is:

> What does 'profound hearing loss' or 'profoundly deaf' or 'severely hearing-impaired' mean as far as *my* child is concerned?

She realises that immediately after diagnosis there can be no exact answer to these questions, but she feels very strongly that there is something that must be made clear to parents at this stage. No matter how the child's hearing loss is described, that child almost certainly has some useful hearing which must be exploited to the full.

Once parents have accepted that there is hearing to be developed, their next question is often, 'How can we help our child to learn to listen?' So many opportunities to help the child to develop skill in listening arise in everyday life if the significant adults in the child's environment act as though they expect the child to hear.

In the early stages, however, it is very difficult for some parents to sustain this belief, if the child is slow to react to sound. In Birkdale School a group of parents of fifty-six hearing-impaired children aged between twelve and sixteen (each child with a hearing loss over 90dB across the speech range), were asked the question, 'How did you feel in the early stages when trying to help your child to learn to listen?' It should be noted that all their children had become good listeners. The responses of this group were very varied:

- 15 per cent saw an immediate improvement in the child's response to sound.
- 28 per cent found a slow but steady improvement in the child's response to sound.
- 32 per cent saw a little change at times, but were very anxious because progress seemed to be so slow.
- 25 per cent saw no progress at all for a period of over two months.

These figures give some idea of the size of the problem in the weeks immediately following the fitting of the child's hearing-aids. A selection of actual responses from the parents carries with it something of the stress that many experience at this time. It is indicative of how much support is needed at the early stages.

A small sample of responses from anxious parents

- 'She was no different whether the aids were on or off for about three months. It seemed a very long time to keep going and seeing nothing.'
- 'For the first few months we had no indication that the hearing-aids helped at all.'
- 'It was right hard at first. It was all giving and no getting. I kept

putting sound into the hearing-aids and got nothing back at all. It was hard to keep going, but it's easier now because he's started to give definite responses to certain sounds.

- 'She showed no reaction for at least four months after having her hearing-aids. We felt like giving up because we felt right stupid, talking away and never any answer. We're glad we kept going because she can even hear the telephone in the room next door now.'

The important thing to realise is that, in spite of such slow beginnings, each of the fifty-six children under discussion learned to make very good use of whatever residual hearing they had and so developed fluent spoken language. In the case of those who were slow to show that they were receiving benefit from their hearing-aids, the picture might have been very different if the parents had not had consistent support at the early stages.

One way in which to help parents who are anxiously waiting to see results, is to draw their attention to all the things that their child *can* do. They should be encouraged to find out what the child enjoys doing and to accompany this with meaningful chatter. Parents need to realise that the listening skill is not something to be *taught* in isolation, but is something to be *developed* in a stimulating environment in which the child is motivated to listen. Although the child should have a variety of auditory experience, it is important to impress upon those dealing with the child that the most important thing for him to hear is *speech*. Through good interaction in play activities many opportunities arise for those involved to use meaningful language about the activities which really interest the child, so motivating him to listen.

Parents should be encouraged to react very positively to any response that the child gives to sound. Children love to please and, if those in the environment show pleasure when hearing-impaired children respond to sound, this will have a reinforcing effect.

The repetitive nature of the daily routine of a young child's life gives ample opportunity for those constantly with the child to talk naturally about things in the immediate environment. It may well be that the professional offering guidance to the family has to demonstrate what is meant by 'talking naturally'. The effect of a lack of normal responses from the child can cause parents to become inhibited and to talk in stilted short phrases, or in single words instead of using a normal flow of language at a normal rate of utterance.

The vocal fun games of early childhood can play an important part at a time when a hearing-impaired child is learning to listen. Parents should be encouraged to make full use of such games, for example Peep Bo routines. The child's attention should be attracted by the calling of his name and not by touching him or by the stamping of feet to cause vibration.

Attention should be drawn to sounds that occur regularly, both in the home and outside, for example, the sound that the washing machine makes when it is working and the fact that it makes no sound when it is switched off. Our lives are full of sound – the telephone, dogs barking, traffic noise etc. and hearing-impaired children should be encouraged not just to become aware of the sounds in their environments, but also to identify their source. Sounds that occur unexpectedly should also be explored. The smashing of a cup or the knocking over of a chair make distinctive sounds and should be identified as they happen. The fact that certain things can be heard whilst others can not, even by hearing people, should be pointed out to hearing-impaired children. Recently, a mother of a little girl with a very severe hearing loss had to explain to her that hair does not make a noise when it falls to the floor during cutting. This little girl, just at the stage of beginning to identify the sounds in her environment, was most insistent that she could hear her hair drop!

It is such a joy to observe a young hearing-impaired child gradually becoming aware of sound. One mother, who had been told at the time of diagnosis that her child did not have sufficient hearing to learn to talk, was greatly encouraged to find her four-year-old able to draw her attention to water running in the kitchen and to the sound of the radio in the car.

Simple noise-making toys should be available for the child to explore and enjoy. The more variety there is, the more varied the child's experience of sound will be. Home made shakers, a hammer toy, a drum, a car with a siren, wooden sticks to hit together etc. are easily available and are but a few of the many things that will help the child to explore the world of sound. Once parents understand what is required it is surprising how resourceful they become in this respect.

Music can play a very significant part in the life of a hearing-impaired child. Parents should be encouraged to sing nursery rhymes into the microphone of the hearing-aids. The child should be encouraged to move to music, and games that call for a response when the music stops should be introduced.

In stories with a repetitive refrain young children learn to anticipate what they will hear next as they become familiar with the story. Such stories provide very valuable listening experience for hearing-impaired children. Recently, the author watched a mother sharing the story of *The Gingerbread Man* with a four-year-old boy whose mean hearing loss across the speech range is 105dB. This little boy took great pleasure in trying to join in the 'Run, run as fast as you can' refrain.

If the child's hearing is to be stimulated to the full, care must be taken to talk within the range of the hearing-aids. When mother and child are engaged in activities around the home the use of a radio system allows more freedom as distance from the microphone is no longer a problem. At the same time, it is very important to ensure that parents are trained to switch off the radio transmitter when not chatting to the child. If this is not done, confusion arises when the child receives information through the transmitter that is not related to the activity in which he is engaged.

Parents can be trained to observe their child's reactions to sound. They often find it helpful to keep an informal record, between guidance sessions, of any interesting responses that the child has made to voice or to other environmental sounds. When they are involved in this way, parents sometimes notice reactions that they might otherwise have missed. As the weeks progress their record often becomes a real source of encouragement to them. Such a record serves another purpose too. Professionals are with children for only such short periods of time that parents' observations can help them to build up a clearer picture of the child's progress in learning to listen.

Factors that detract from the use of residual hearing

When seeking to create a certain type of environment it is always important to consider factors that might produce negative results or which might work in some way against the goal to be achieved. In the case of residual hearing this is an area that has received scant attention when the development of listening skills has been under discussion.

Transistorised hearing-aids became freely available in Britain through the National Health Service in the late 1950s, and a great wave of optimism swept through the field of 'deaf education' as it was then known. In many instances this optimism has been justified and, today, young men and women with severe and profound hearing losses can be found in all walks of life, fully integrated into normal society. This is possible for them because of the fluency and intelligibility of spoken language which they have developed. This, in turn, has come about because of the stimulation of their residual hearing in an environment in which they have interacted with people who have communicated with them in normal spoken language.

In sharp contrast to these young people, however, are others with similar hearing losses, access to hearing-aids and ability, whose oral communication skills have not developed sufficiently for them to feel at home in society at large. The contrast in these two groups of young hearing-impaired people cannot be attributed wholly to degree of hearing loss; innate factors such as intelligence or to social class background. When comparisons are being made a significant factor which is often overlooked is their early 'listening environment'. The problem seems to be that it is very difficult to prove statistically that one feature of an environment detracts more than another from the full use of a hearing-impaired child's residual hearing. In practice, however, those who have worked in a truly auditory system can produce many examples, related to elements in the early environment, which seem to throw light on certain features that appear to have an inhibiting effect on the maximum use of hearing. Some of the factors which may detract from the use of hearing are:

- Late diagnosis with consequent late issue of hearing-aids.
- Insufficient maintenance of hearing-aids.
- Unfavourable listening conditions.
- Too much emphasis on visual cues.

Late diagnosis with consequent late issue of hearing-aids

Children do not live in a vacuum and if residual hearing is not stimulated early, hearing-impaired children will seek to come to terms with their environment by visual means. Once they have come to rely on their eyes as the 'way in', those working with them in a truly auditory oral approach find it very difficult to stimulate these children to become as fully auditorily aware as they could have been had they had appropriate amplification from the earliest possible age. Without doubt, amongst the many hearing-impaired children with severe and profound hearing losses, known to the author, those whose voices have the most natural rhythm and intonation are those who have worn hearing-aids regularly from before the age of one year.

It is not surprising to find that children who have had hearing-aids from a young age but who have not worn them consistently, often present in a very similar way to those who received their hearing-aids late due to the late diagnosis of their hearing loss. This seems to indicate that time lost in the stimulation of residual hearing is time that cannot easily be regained.

Insufficient maintenance of hearing-aids

When hearing-aids have undetected faults, or when they have to be sent away for repair, without there being an adequate replacement available, the continuity of auditory experience is interrupted and the child's listening experience is reduced. This can cause confusion to an inexperienced listener: auditory signals tend to become ignored and preference given to the more constant visual cues. As a result, maximum use is not made of residual hearing. At a practical level, those dealing with hearing-impaired children from a wide geographical area can, on occasion, pin-point poor hearing-aid maintenance in a specific local area by noticing that the children reaching school age from that area have poor listening skills.

Unfavourable listening conditions

All those encouraging hearing-impaired children to use hearing-aids should themselves take time to listen through the prescribed aids in the situation in which the children will wear them. Noisy, reverberant rooms with, perhaps a television blaring in the background, are not conducive to the development of listening skills! Parents need advice on how best to adapt their home situation to provide realistic conditions which will allow the child to enjoy the experience of wearing hearing-aids and which will ensure that the best possible pattern of sound is being received.

Listening conditions are an important factor to bear in mind when considering the placement of a pre-school hearing-impaired child in a nursery school or playgroup. At times, parents report that a child is reluctant to wear hearing-aids when going into such a setting. They often attribute this reluctance to the child's sensitivity to looking different from other children. In reality, the root of the problem may well be the very noisy conditions within the pre-school setting. The use of some form of radio system can often improve the situation in such cases.

Where there is goodwill and good cooperation between the staff of the nursery school or playgroup and those responsible for the placement of the hearing-impaired child, a real effort is sometimes made to improve the listening conditions. All young children, not only those who have hearing losses, benefit from carpeted areas, curtains and perhaps even a lowered ceiling in the areas in which they play. Funds have to be raised to make such adaptations, and through real involvement in fund-raising activities the parents of a hearing-impaired child are often greatly helped. The author has noticed parents who had been very tense about their hearing-impaired child relax, noticeably, as they have worked side by side with the parents of children who have normal hearing. They have discovered that some of the behaviour that has been worrying them in their child is to be found in children without hearing losses and is, in fact, age-related rather than due to hearing loss.

Too much emphasis on visual cues

In pre-hearing-aid days it was necessary to look upon a hearing-impaired child's eyes as *substitutes* for his ears. All sorts of practices were adopted which were thought to make lipreading easier for the child. Many of these were quite foreign to the early language learning environment of a young child with normal hearing. Tradition dies hard and many of these practices remain today, in environments in which hearing-impaired children have been issued with hearing-aids. It must again be noted that an auditory oral approach does not deny the hearing-impaired child the opportunity to lipread, but it does not place emphasis on visual cues, nor does it adopt the practices identified below.

Deliberate drawing of attention to the lips

This practice may occur in a variety of ways. A speaker may point to the area of the lips and ask the children to 'watch', whereas children in a truly auditory oral programme would be asked to 'listen'. Objects may be held up at the side of the lips in an attempt to develop lipreading skills. This practice often has the added effect of an over-emphasis on vocabulary in the language which is offered to hearing-impaired children. It certainly interrupts the normal non-verbal behaviour between adult and child.

Lip movements may be exaggerated in an attempt to make lipreading easier. This usually has the effect of slowing down the normal rate of utterance, as well as encouraging abnormal facial expression. When the normal rate of utterance is broken, a very valuable auditory cue is lost.

The positioning of hearing-impaired toddlers in high chairs for 'guidance' sessions so that they are on eye level opposite a sitting adult, is another practice that, albeit unconsciously, may lead to an over emphasis on vision. 'Get down to eye level' was an instruction issued to many teachers in training for work with young hearing-impaired children in the pre-hearing-aid days. As a result, teachers and the parents that they guided almost always dropped down to the height of the children when communicating with them. The author saw this practice recently in a situation where a mother and child were actually in touch by means of a very effective radio hearing-aid system. Practices like these must be questioned in the light of improved hearing-aid technology if the benefits of the new hearing-aids are not to be lost.

The availability of manual systems of communication

Systems of communication such as cued speech, finger-spelling or any of the sign languages rely on reception through the *eye*. When one of these is being used, the sense of vision which is unimpaired (in most cases) undoubtedly takes over from the impaired sense – hearing – at the early stages. As a result, the hearing-impaired child's motivation to listen is reduced. The poor voice quality, with resultant poor speech intelligibility of so many children in educational settings which use any form of manual support, gives cause for concern to many who work within these settings. The author, on recent visits to Total Communication Programmes for hearing-impaired children in several countries, heard time and again the words, 'If only we could do something about the speech'. The problem is inherent in the system because of its emphasis on vision, and recent work of Markides (1988) supports this claim. In a comparative study involving two matched groups of hearing-impaired children Markides found that:

(*a*) The auditory-oral approach produced better speech intelligibility than total communication; and

(*b*) The speech intelligibility of the hearing-impaired children who changed from the auditory-oral approach to total communication deteriorated significantly over a period of 5 years.

Too slow a rate of utterance

A fallacy that has remained from pre-hearing-aid days is that lipreading is made easier if speech is greatly slowed down. This may well be the case for those who were brought up to expect it to be so, but the argument does not hold for today's hearing-impaired children who have been fitted with appropriate hearing-aids and who have been spoken to, from the start, at a normal rate of utterance.

One multiple-handicapped young man with a profound hearing loss who can be seen on video-tape (Clark, 1985) certainly does not look for slower speech. One of the significant features of this excerpt of video-tape is the speed at which the communication takes place. While he was still at school he once asked the author, 'Speak a bit quicker please. The faster you talk the more I get in an eyeful.'

So much is to be learned from this young man. On account of his hearing loss he is most certainly reliant on lipreading to back up the imperfect auditory patterns which he receives through his hearing-aids. In an auditory oral system, however, he has developed such a good command of colloquial language that he is not attempting to lipread every word in a sentence any more than a good reader reads every word on the page of a book. His aim is to share meaning with his conversational partner and he is sufficiently at home in the medium of spoken language to be able to be relaxed enough in the conversational situation to lipread patterns as they flow along accompanied by all the auditory cues upon which he is so dependent. For his understanding of the message he is dependent upon normal rhythm and stress patterns that evolve in speech which is spoken at a normal rate and which he is partly hearing and partly lipreading.

Conclusion

Hearing-impaired children will learn to listen best if those responsible for their management really believe that it is possible for them to receive positive help from hearing-aids, and if they ensure that these hearing-aids can be worn all day and maintained in such a way that the children receive a consistent pattern of sound. The environment must be managed in such a way that the children are expected and motivated to listen. It must also be critically appraised to ensure that no factors within it detract from the use of hearing-aids.

5

Language Through the Daily Routine of the Home

> *Everything that happens in a child's daily life is a potential subject for the sort of talk that facilitates attention, interpretation, and evaluation, but parents differ in the use they make of these opportunities.*
>
> (Wells, 1983)

One of the main responsibilities of the professional seeking to guide the parents of a hearing-impaired child through the early years, is to help them to use the opportunities which arise out of daily life, to facilitate language learning. If the task is approached from this angle, it is possible to avoid the pitfall of making parents feel that their child learns language best when they sit down and 'teach' it, or that teachers know better than they do how to help a hearing-impaired child to develop language. Pugh and De'Ath (1984) warn that unless care is taken, professionals can indeed have the effect of undermining the self-confidence of parents who can be intimidated by the 'expertise' of the professional.

It is important that parents do not feel that the professional has all the answers and will tell them exactly what to do with their hearing-impaired child as if they were following a recipe. Home visits by a professional should not be looked upon as the times of the week when the child 'does language'. If this attitude develops there is a tendency for parents to opt out and to wait for the professional to 'make it happen'.

Parents must become active partners in the effort to create a language-enabling environment. Professionals can best help them to do this by discussing the daily routine of the home and pointing out how this can provide a rich source of language. Parents who come to understand that their normal daily life does not have to come to a halt while their hearing-impaired child is 'taught' language are likely to learn to involve their child in everyday routines and to accompany their joint activity with meaningful chatter. Professionals need to be ready to support parents and to encourage them in such a way that they develop the confidence to trust the way in which they feel comfortable when interacting with their child.

No one theorist or practitioner has, as yet, produced a wholly acceptable explanation of the process by which any young children develop communicative skills which enable them to converse fluently in their mother tongue and so share meaning with those around them. And yet, at no time in history has more study been directed towards discovering how children develop conversational competence. In the past decade or so a common emphasis is to be found in many of the studies in the field of early child language. The works of Bruner (1983), de Villiers and de Villiers (1979), Wells (1986) and Wood *et al.* (1986) all lay stress on the important part parents play in the language development of their children as they interact with them every day in the home. It now seems clear in relation to the development of competent communication skills, that whatever innate capacity a child has, it can only be fully realised if the significant adults in the environment (usually the parents) interact with the child in such a way as to promote two-way communication that allows for meaning to be shared. In the early years particularly, then, it is the parents who must shoulder the main responsibility for providing support for the child's developing language skills. The home can provide an environment that no other pre-school placement can match. An interesting study by Tizard and Hughes (1984) found that interaction between children (with normal hearing) and the staff of nursery schools was less linguistically motivating than that between children and their mothers at home.

There is no reason to suppose that a child born with impaired hearing is not predisposed to develop language in a way similar to a child with normal hearing. Longitudinal video-taped records of children with severe and profound hearing losses who are being brought up on an auditory oral approach, show them to be passing through the normal stages of linguistic development in the same way as their hearing counterparts, albeit at a slower rate. In the case of these hearing-impaired children, however, the quality of the linguistic support provided by the home is all important because of the reduced auditory cues. When considering the interaction that the young hearing-impaired children enjoy with those in their environment, it is helpful to study different periods of the early years of their lives.

The period prior to diagnosis

Few children have their hearing loss diagnosed before the age of nine months (many are much older) and therefore, in most cases they have been exposed to all the normal mother-child routines until at least that age. The fact that some good foundations for language learning have been laid down during this pre-diagnosis period is all too often forgotten both by parents and those professionals involved with the family after the identification of the hearing loss. Although much of the auditory component of this early communicative behaviour has been missing prior to the issue of a hearing-aid, established routines have laid certain foundations upon which language can be built.

In the familiar environment of the home a fairly regular routine evolves. Its regularity lends itself to repetition and so many opportunities are afforded the young child to have the same experiences again and again. Within such a routine the child begins to make connections between certain events and those that come before or after them. In this way the child develops the ability to be able to predict what will happen next – a very important basis for communication. Babies are not completely dependent upon auditory cues to enable them to follow such routines.

In the first few months of life there is a lot of close physical contact between mother and baby. As mothers hold babies they talk to them about whatever is holding their interest at the time, or about their body language. At such times babies often watch the face of the mother. Although what is said may not be heard because of the hearing loss, facial expression carries a lot of meaning, for example, when a baby is about to put something into his mouth his mother may be seen to shake her head and to scowl as she says, 'Don't put that in your mouth. It's dirty.' The non-verbal elements of the mother's behaviour carry meaning to the child.

Another significant feature of a child's early linguistic environment is the way in which a mother treats her child's behaviour as if it really did have meaning, for example, a little eight-month-old boy was very restless on his mother's lap. The mother picked him up to stand him on his feet, saying as he did so, 'Well, you want to stand up today, do you?' In a situation like this, a child with a significant hearing loss who has not yet been issued with a hearing-aid would not hear the verbal element in the mother's response to his behaviour, but there would be an awareness that mother had understood his discomfort and had done something about it.

Turn taking is a basic element in a conversation. It is established very early on in a child's linguistic development. To begin with it is regulated by the mother or other care-giver, who gives way to any utterance that the child makes and treats it like a turn in a conversation. Video-tape excerpts can show this so clearly. To demonstrate just how naturally this process develops, the author used an example of a mother with a four-month-old baby girl, in which the mother can be seen giving way to the child's vocalisations (Clark, 1985). A child with an, as yet, undetected hearing loss, would have his early utterances treated in the same way as a baby with normal hearing, in this respect.

To draw attention to the positive input that the young hearing-impaired child has had prior to the diagnosis of the hearing loss, is in no way to underestimate the extent of the handicap or the effect that it has on the child's developing language. It does serve, however, to focus the attention of the parents on what has been right in the early environment of the child at a time when they may be experiencing very negative feelings about the role that they themselves have played so far.

The period around diagnosis – parents and professionals becoming partners

One of the problems associated with making parents aware of the presence of a hearing loss in their young child is that they may come to think of that child as very 'different' and as a child who needs to be treated in a 'special way', particularly in relation to language learning. From the point of diagnosis onward, therefore, it is important for parents to be in touch with experienced professionals who will guide and support them at this difficult time. Gradually, a partnership must develop that will have as its basis the common desire to help the hearing-impaired child to reach his full potential in every area of life.

One of the first tasks for the professional is to encourage the parents to go on enjoying their child – to point out to them that they will never have these actual days again and that each day is important in the development of their child. If the parents are really encouraged to do this they will, in all probability, relax and quite naturally begin to provide a normal language learning environment in the process.

Professionals working with the parents of newly diagnosed hearing-impaired children should be able to identify the pre-verbal routines of normal mother-child behaviour, referred to earlier in this chapter. Parents need to be reminded that they have, in fact, been communicating with their child prior to the diagnosis and that they must now go on doing so in a similar way, although they are aware of the presence of a hearing loss.

At this time, when most parents are still in a state of shock, there is a tendency for all sorts of abnormal practices to creep in. Without help, they may begin to treat the child so differently that the linguistic environment that they are providing becomes very different from that experienced by a child with normal hearing. It is no easy task to intervene positively and to win the confidence of parents at such a time, but it is very worth while for professionals to persevere, as this is when firm foundations are being laid for the child's future development.

Involving the parents in the management of the hearing-aids is a starting point from which good rapport can grow. Using Pollack's (1970) concept of a 'hearing age' often proves helpful. Parents can easily come to understand that, in the case of children with severe and profound hearing losses, almost all the auditory element of the child's pre-hearing-aid linguistic experience has been missed. It is useful to explain that a child aged two years and six months has a 'hearing age' of only one year, if the hearing-aids were not fitted until the child was aged eighteen months. This concept often helps to take some of the pressure off parents who are over-anxious for early results. It highlights the need for them to continue the early mother-child routines for a longer period of time so that the child can now experience them with the help of the auditory cues which his hearing-aids will supply.

Those whose hearing loss has been diagnosed very late have additional problems. Wood *et al.* (1986) has outlined some of the difficulties of trying to establish the type of language learning environment that a baby enjoys naturally, for older more mature children. Parents in this position need special help from the professional responsible for guidance. Above all, they need reassurance that it can be done, if they are sensitive to the needs and interests of their child.

Some parents may be difficult to help because they have lost faith in professionals, on account of delay in the diagnosis of their child's hearing loss at a time when they themselves were sure that the child had a hearing problem. In the author's experience, this situation is quite common. In the school year 1981–82 thirty-eight young children were brought on first visits to Birkdale School. The parents of twenty-one of these had had difficulty in having their suspicions of a hearing loss in their child confirmed. Valuable time had been lost and in some cases resentment against professionals was quite strong. It takes time to regain the trust of parents in this position and to help them to relax, because the frustration they have experienced usually makes them tense. Although professionals are aware that time lost can never be fully regained, the message which anxious parents need is that something very positive can now be done *every day* as they interact with their child in the familiar environment of the home. These parents, especially, should be reminded that much of what they have already been doing naturally with the child has been helpful. The knowledge that their efforts to date have been worthwhile encourages them further.

At the time of adjustment to having a hearing-impaired child, it is necessary for parents to have the opportunity to meet teenagers or young adults who have impaired hearing, but who have developed fluent oral communication skills. Time and again parents have told the author that what helped them most when they were trying to come to terms with their child's hearing loss was meeting children of secondary school age with hearing losses similar to that of their child and discovering that they could chat with them easily. On finding this they came to realise that these young people had developed enough language to cope with all the subjects on a normal school timetable. This helped them to set realistic expectations for their own child. An experience such as this helps parents to realise that 'Language is for meeting people: for forming social relationships: for interacting with others.' (Cook, 1979)

Nothing can take the place of face to face contact with orally competent young hearing-impaired people. If, however, for any reason, such contact cannot be arranged, then excerpts of video-tapes can go some way towards meeting this need. Once parents have seen the normality of language that can be achieved they are far more likely to treat their newly diagnosed hearing-impaired child along normal lines.

The period after the initial counselling

Once parents have had the initial counselling and the hearing-impaired child has been issued with hearing-aids, the family has to settle back into a day to day routine which takes account of the child's hearing loss, but which is not dominated by it. It must be made clear to the parents that the professional offering guidance is easily available and will maintain regular contact, but that the prime responsibility for encouraging the child to listen and for the provision of a stimulating environment, is theirs.

The hearing loss is likely to be there for life, and therefore, parents must assess the needs of the whole family as they seek to adjust to those of the hearing-impaired child. The special needs of this child should be discussed with the family as a whole, in such a way as to involve all members. It is important that brothers and sisters should feel that a proper balance is being kept between their own needs and those of the child with a hearing loss. The extended family and close friends can offer such a lot of support if they can be brought to an understanding of the situation. It is, however, important that those interacting with the hearing-impaired child are not over protective and that they do not anticipate his every need so well that the child's motivation to develop the language he needs to make things happen is reduced.

In normal daily life, from waking up to going to bed, there are opportunities for interaction between parent and child. Parents should be encouraged to talk to the child as clothes go on in the morning, chatting about the various items of clothing and the order in which they go on. Setting the table for meals can be a repetitive routine which fosters confidence in the child. The child will know, from context at first, what is expected and then gradually, through the repetition of the activity, the child will come to associate the phrases that the mother uses with the various routines.

Young children love to help and to be involved with their parents in real tasks around the house. Young hearing-impaired children are no exception and can learn so much if they are allowed to help with the daily routine jobs. The following transcript of an interaction between Karen, aged two-and-a-half (mean hearing loss 110dB across the speech range) and her mother illustrates this well.

Mother and Karen are standing at the front door, having just waved off father and the two other children in the family.

Mother	Come on then, Karen. That's them all gone. Daddy's gone to work, Jamie's gone to school and so has Babs. *(Taking Karen's hand and shivering)* Let's close this door and keep out the cold.
Karen	*(Shivering to imitate mother)* –old.
Mother	Yes, isn't it cold? Let's warm our hands on this radiator.
Karen	–O.
Mother	Well, it's hot, but it's not that hot, so you don't need to make a fuss. *(Karen looks puzzled)* Anyway if we get on with our work we won't need to heat our hands. *(Pointing to the breakfast table)* Can you carry these things into the kitchen?
Karen	*(Nods and picks up packet of cornflakes. Drops them.)* Oh –ee!
Mother	Oh dear, what a mess! Never mind. Let's clear it up.

(Karen dashes for a brush.)
(Mother brings a small shovel.)

Mother	Brush them on to my shovel. Go on. *(Pointing to the cornflakes on the floor.)*

(Karen tries but looks to mother for help.)

Mother	Will I help you?

(Karen nods. When cornflakes are on the shovel Karen opens the packet.)

Mother	Oh no! Not in there, you silly billy! These are all dirty now – look!

(Karen wriggles her nose and nods, pointing to the rubbish bin.)

Mother	That's right, in there – into the bin.

(Karen lifts the lid off the bin.)

Mother	Thank you.

This interchange took place in the space of only four minutes, but what a lot happened in that short time! Karen was wearing her hearing-aids, having put them on when getting up. Her mother's chatter was wholly natural and at a normal rate. She spoke regardless of whether Karen was looking at her or not. Meaning was certainly shared between this little girl and her mother. It is worthwhile pausing and considering just a little of the experience that Karen gained in such a short time.

It would be reasonable to assume that waving father and the other children off is part of a regular morning routine. Karen is offered an explanation of where the other members of the family go each day, and a comment on the weather follows with a natural gesture from the mother which certainly carries meaning. The mother then goes on to explain that doors are shut to keep the cold out and that radiators are places on which cold hands may be warmed. The rather dramatic withdrawal of Karen's hand from the radiator is treated in a very matter-of-fact way and the topic is changed smartly. Karen tunes in to her mother's request and, in her eagerness to help, drops the packet of cornflakes. She attempts to use a very normal colloquial expression as she says, 'Oh –ee.' Her mother immediately responds with, 'Oh dear!' thus giving her a correct model of what she attempted to say, and enlarges on it with a further comment, 'What a mess!' At the same time she is careful to reassure Karen that nothing serious has happened and she offers a practical solution. Karen is quick to weigh up the situation and dashes for a brush. She takes a little time to respond to her mother's suggestion that she should brush the cornflakes on to the shovel and then finds herself in difficulty because of the size of her brush. She appeals, with a meaningful look, to her mother, who responds straight away with the offer to help. Karen accepts this with a nod and then considers putting the spilt cornflakes back into the packet. Mother's expression and tone of voice leave her in no doubt that this is not to happen. She looks round for another solution. By pointing her finger she suggests the dustbin and her mother happily agrees to this and thanks Karen for lifting off the lid for her.

An experience such as this really does present a young child with an opportunity to learn language through living. The lives of young children are full of such moments as they follow adults around the house, so long as they are allowed to be involved in the activities in which the adults are engaged. Parents seldom realise what effective educators they are. The problem is that the moment their attention is drawn to it, they are inclined to think that they should act like teachers! It is important that those offering guidance to the parents of young hearing-impaired children do not fall into the trap of under-valuing what parents actually do naturally. If this happens they are inclined to try to turn parents into teachers, and a great deal of the normal spontaneity of the language which parents use naturally with their children can be lost.

Cooking, washing, ironing and general housework are essential parts of every household routine and offer endless opportunities. Young children and their parents who enjoy activities together in this way build up a great volume of *shared experience*. This is an important basis for communication. Within such an environment mothers come to know their children so well that they can nearly always work out what it is that their child wants to convey. This point is missed by those who insist that the parents of young hearing-impaired children cannot communicate with them unless they use signs.

Not all regular family routines take place within the home. Shopping must be part of the experience of almost every young child. Supermarkets provide such wonderful linguistic opportunities! There are choices to be made and explanations to be given. There are people to be met and conversations to be held in real life situations. When Wells (1985) analysed the data in his Bristol study he found that if conversations were to extend over a number of turns at the early stages, the adult had to make the effort to understand the child's intended meaning and to extend it in terms which the child could understand. Children can be very motivated to get meaning across when in a situation that is not quite so familiar as the home, and so the parent is provided with an opportunity to engage in a true sharing of meaning which extends over several turns. The following dialogue, which took place in a supermarket, illustrates this point well. Four-year-old Janet who has a very severe hearing loss (90–95dB across the speech range) was sitting in a trolley as her mother went from one area to another in their local supermarket. Mother stopped the trolley by the shelves on which the biscuits were displayed and the conversation went like this:

Mother   *(Holding a packet of cheese biscuits)* Neil wants these. He likes cheese biscuits. These are for Neil. *(Pointing to Janet)* You can choose a packet that you'd like.
(Janet laughs and points to a packet of chocolate biscuits.)
Mother   These ones? *(Lifting up the packet.)*
(Janet nods)
Mother   These are chocolate biscuits. I like chocolate biscuits too. So does Daddy.
Janet   Pip.
Mother   Pardon?
Janet   Pip.
Mother   *(Shrugs shoulders and turns palms of hands upwards)* Pip?
(Janet nods)
Mother   Pip's at home. We don't bring dogs into food shops. Look there are no dogs here.
Janet   Pip bi—it.
Mother   *(Same gesture as before)* Oh you want biscuits for Pip. They're not here. You don't get <u>dog</u> biscuits beside <u>our</u> biscuits.
Janet   Pip, Pip. *(as Mother begins to move the trolley)*
Mother   It's all right. We'll get some biscuits for Pip here. Look, here are Pip's biscuits.
Janet   Big one.
Mother   *(Smiles, nods and points to a packet of dog biscuits)* Yes, Pip has a bigger packet than you.

This transcript illustrates so well how a mother can negotiate meaning and keep a conversation going in a most natural way in an everyday situation. It shows that even when a child has a very severe hearing loss, if mother and child are really accustomed to sharing experiences, they come to expect to understand each other. The mother can be seen here to take Janet's non-verbal responses, for example, her nods, as turns in the conversation to which she attributes meaning. They understand each other so well that, as a result, when a misunderstanding arises, they negotiate meaning until the misunderstanding is satisfactorily cleared up. It is through such experiences that hearing-impaired children develop the ability to discover the needs of their conversational partners and also develop the confidence to persevere until meaning really has been shared.

Young children love to have attention from their fathers, and it is important that routines are not always built up with just the mother. The father is apt to be someone who seems to come and go a lot in the life of the young child. On the whole, because of the work situation, fathers do seem to have less contact with their young children than mothers. In the case of a hearing-impaired child, it is important that the father has as much contact as possible so that he is able to tune his language naturally to the stage of the child, as the mother does through her daily routines.

Tucker *et al.* (1983) who compared maternal and paternal input to young hearing-impaired children found that, on the whole, fathers talked less and used more single words. They suggest that, to some extent, this is because fathers have not had as much guidance as mothers after the diagnosis of the hearing loss. Professionals dealing with the families of hearing-impaired children need to be particularly alert to this problem. Fathers have so much to offer, especially if they are made aware of how important their contribution can be to the developing language of their child. At the time of writing, the author was working in Turkey in a culture where it is common for both

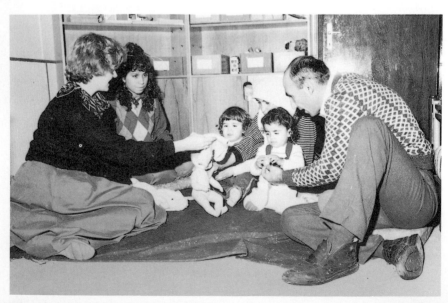

The whole family involved in a guidance session

parents to come to each guidance session with their hearing-impaired child. In this situation fathers often take the initiative and the dominant role during the time spent with the professional. No comparative study has been undertaken, but it does appear that the responsibility for providing a stimulating linguistic environment is more evenly shared when both parents receive regular guidance. It should be added that Turkish fathers of children with normal hearing are not so involved, and it does seem, therefore, that it is the guidance offered which makes the difference.

There are so many practical situations which the children find exciting and in which one or both parents can be involved, for example, things to be mended, cars to be washed, or jobs to be done in the garden. When young hearing-impaired children have the opportunity to share in these, a wide range of meaningful experiences provides the basis for much new language learning, if the various activities are accompanied by meaningful chatter. The simple routines of everyday life, then, are probably the greatest resource that parents can tap in relation to the developing language of a hearing-impaired child.

= 6 =
Language Through Other Activities with Parents

> *Children and adults learn from each other and enrich each other's lives.*
>
> (Bruce, 1987)

Bruce's words can be particularly true in the case of a handicapped child. As parents gradually become aware of the particular needs of that child, a very special relationship can develop between parent and child – not one that excludes the needs of the rest of the family, but rather one that may enrich the life of the whole family.

As those responsible for guiding parents of hearing-impaired children in the pre-school years seek to make them aware of the linguistic needs of the child, they can lead them into exploring their environment in a way that parents may not previously have considered. Everyday life offers such a wide range of opportunities. It is so satisfying to hear the parent of a hearing-impaired child say, 'Do you know, we had a great time doing that together. I enjoyed it as much as Amy did. I've never rubbed bark before, so that's something we've both learned and I'll show the others how to do it, too, now.'

Involvement in an activity which leads parents to such enjoyment and satisfaction has certainly not come from deliberate formal attempts to 'teach the child language'. It has evolved, rather, from the parent's sharing some real activity with the child, in which both have been so involved that the child has been treated as a true conversational partner. In these circumstances much will have been learned about the process of communication.

Recently, another parent was heard to say 'All of us know a lot more nowadays and that's because of our Karen. It's funny because she's the deaf one, and yet it's because of her that we've all begun to look around and explore things like we never did before.' Opening up the possibility for this to happen is a vital part of the work of the professional involved with the family of a hearing-impaired child in the early years. Such an approach, not only fosters good interaction between those in the environment and the child, but it also ensures that very positive attitudes develop in relation to the hearing-impaired child.

Environments vary from area to area. It is neither possible nor necessary to produce an exhaustive list of ways in which they may be explored to the advantage of a hearing-impaired child. This chapter deals with a few of the avenues that are open to those who are interacting daily with young children. None demands expensive materials, but all depend upon the active involvement of an interested parent or care-giver.

Play

All young children need to play and it is important that the parents of hearing-impaired children recognise this and allow time for play in day to day living. It is sad to meet a hearing-impaired child whose parents have been so anxious that he should be taught to speak, that insufficient time has been allowed for play. Such a child loses opportunities that can never be regained – so many of a child's needs are met in play. Parents, and the professionals guiding them, must, therefore plan the hearing-impaired child's day in such a way as to allow ample time for play.

Right from the start it is important for parents to realise that play material does not always need to consist of commercially-produced toys. Homes are full of natural play objects, such as a bag of coloured clothes pegs or empty cardboard cartons, and young children should have the opportunity to explore and experiment with these simple materials. The home is a rich source of noise-making objects: saucepan lids to bang together, large dried beans to pour in and out of a tin, dried peas sealed into an empty washing-up bottle to act as a shaker etc.

Parents need to be made aware that there are times to leave children to experiment on their own and times to become involved in their play. Crowe (1983), talking about the play of children in general, says:

> If we break in uninvited to try to use play for 'educational purposes' we defeat both nature's ends and our own.

It is very tempting for the parents of hearing-impaired children to do just what Crowe warns against. Aware of the real need of the child to have opportunities to learn language, they are inclined to want to fill every minute with chatter. As a result, a child's exploratory play is sometimes unnecessarily interrupted. It requires skill to keep the balance between good non-intrusive interaction and too little interaction. Fairly sound advice to offer is that the child should usually be left alone if absorbed in a particular activity, but that the parent should be ready to join in if the child looks up as if inviting the parent to do so. Advice along these lines generally helps parents to observe and to become responsive to the child while, at the same time, they learn not to impose their own ideas too much while the child is playing freely.

Professionals, with wide experience of the play of young children, can create situations which serve as models for parents anxious to provide a good language learning environment for a hearing-impaired child. Parents need to understand that it is the sharing of an activity, with the consequent sharing of meaning that matters, not the teaching of specific vocabulary related to the activity. At the same time, professionals must guard against the temptation to do all the work with the child. Young children are fun to work with and a session spent interacting with the hearing-impaired child often gives a greater sense of satisfaction to the professional than one in which time is spent observing the interaction of parent and child, especially if this requires much modification. The importance of advising parents in the light of observation of their style of interaction with the hearing-impaired child cannot be over-emphasised.

The professional can do much to heighten the powers of observation of parents. When attention is drawn to some new stage that the child has reached, or to something interesting that the child has done, the parents feel a sense of satisfaction and of success and are consequently motivated to further interaction and awareness.

Meers (1976) makes an interesting observation about exploratory play. She claims that young children learn the names of things that they act upon and that act themselves, for example, building blocks, balls, cars that go etc. She goes on to point out that they are not interested in things that are 'just there', for example, tables, chairs, etc. It is true that as children experiment with materials around them, they are more often interested in what these things *do*, than in what they *are called*. The author was watching a twenty-month-old toddler with normal hearing recently whose play certainly bore this theory out. He dropped his teddy, picked it up and put it in a truck. His commentary went as follows:

Oh dear, fall down.
Pick 'im up.
Put 'im on.
Wind it up.
'way you go.

This whole sequence was concerned with action. If parents and care-givers can enter into the spirit of the play, they will provide the type of commentary that uses a high proportion of action words.

In the case of hearing-impaired children more exposure to language is necessary because the auditory cues they receive are imperfect. There is no doubt that wise intervention at the right time, when a child is showing interest in an activity or object, can certainly facilitate learning. The following transcript serves to illustrate this point. Jonathan, aged two years and three months has a hearing loss across the speech range of over 100dB. He and his mother were sitting on the floor as he played purposefully with a hammer toy. Meaning was certainly being shared and there was lots of natural repetition of language connected with the activity.

Jonathan	*(Looking up at mother)* Da da.
Mother	That's right. You hammer away.
Jonathan	*(Striking a peg with the hammer)* Da da.
Mother	*(Pointing to another peg)* Hammer that one now.
Jonathan	Da da da.
Mother	*(Pointing to a different peg)* What about that one this time.
Jonathan	*(Trying to hit the peg that mother indicated, but missing)* Da.
Mother	*(Laughing)* Oh, you missed it. Never mind try again.
Jonathan	*(Laughing, misses peg again)* Da da.
Mother	Dear me, you missed it again. Shall I have a go? *(Holding out her hand for the hammer)*.
(Jonathan nods and hands over the hammer.)	
Mother	Look, I hammered that one. There's only one left. Can you hammer it? Look! That one there.
Jonathan	Aw aw *(hits last peg)*.
Mother	Jolly good. Yes, they've all gone now.
Jonathan	Aw aw. *(Laughing, shrugs shoulders and points to toy with upturned hands.)*
Mother	Let's put it away now. We've finished hammering. *(Hands toy to Jonathan and looks towards the cupboard.)*
(Jonathan nods and carries toy to the cupboard.)	

Interactions of this kind, in play situations, build up the expectation of both parent and child that each will understand the other, and so the very foundations of communication are laid. Such a lot happened in that short exchange. Right at the start Jonathan's glance invited his mother to join in and she was quick to accept the invitation. Although Jonathan has no recognisable words, as yet, turn taking is well-established and the interchange flows along just like a conversation. Using conventional non-verbal gestures, like pointing, his mother cued Jonathan in to the suggestions she offered and his responses indicated that he understood her meaning. It is interesting to note how Jonathan picked up the emotional atmosphere created by his mother. When she laughed, he laughed in his next turn. Note, too, what a good listener his mother was. Whenever Jonathan altered his vocalisation from, 'Da da' to 'Aw aw', his mother picked this up and attributed meaning to it by saying, 'Yes, they've all gone now.' At the end of such an interaction both parent and child have a feeling of satisfaction and such an experience fosters the desire for further conversation.

Fathers often engage in a completely different kind of activity from those in which mothers and children participate. They can often be observed involving the child in rough and tumble physical play in a situation in which both are very relaxed. One father, on coming home from work, greeted his four-and-a-half-year-old little boy, Paul, in the following way. (Paul has a hearing loss of 110dB across the speech range.)

Father	*(Holding out his arms)* Come on then. Come to Daddy. What have you been doing all day?
Paul	*(Running into his father's arms)* Up.
Father	Oh, you want to go up. High up?

(Paul nods and squeals with delight.)

Father	*(Holds Paul up above his head and looks up at him)* Hullo there.
Paul	Down.
Father	You're no sooner up than you want down. Let's turn you upside down. *(Turns Paul over as he lowers him.)*
Paul	*(Squeals with excitement and delight)* 'gain.

And so the game went on for quite some time. The fun and laughter on the part of both Paul and his father showed just how much each was enjoying the other's company – another good basis for communication.

It is important to have a range of interesting materials in the environment. There are so many available that it is impossible to mention them all here but play dough and bubble solution are two examples of substances which can be exploited in many ways. Through shared interest and involvement with materials of this kind, children not only build up their communication skills as they learn language, but also absorb information about the properties of the things in their environment.

All sorts of opportunities for imaginative and dramatic play present themselves. Children love to dress up and to imitate and enlarge upon the behaviour of the adults around them. Parents and others can foster this by supplying appropriate props and by becoming involved themselves, always taking care, however, not to dominate the situation. A very fine example of a parent doing this with her four-year-old daughter, Kate, who has a profound hearing loss, can be found on the video-tape of the Teaching Pack, *Laying the Foundations* (Clark, 1985).

As children grow older, simple games with rules play a part, as they usually provide ample opportunity for repetition and also for turn taking. Large floor skittles (made from empty washing-up bottles) provided four-and-a-half-year-old James (mean hearing loss across the speech range, 105dB) with many opportunities to use his developing language skills.

James	*(To mother)* 'oll a ball.
Mother	*(Throwing the ball up)* Like that?
James	*(Taking the ball and rolling it)* No. 'i 'at.

Mother	I see. How many did you knock down? Let's count.
Mother and James	One, two three four.
Mother	Four.
James	Yes. You turn now.
Mother	Oh, it's my turn again?
(James nods)	
Mother	*(Rolling the ball)* Good! How many have I knocked down?
Mother and James	One, two three, four.
Mother	Now I'm the same as you.
(James nods.)	*(Rolls the ball)* 'nother go.

This game lasted for twenty minutes. A very interesting feature of it was that James was taking the initiative in organising it for quite a large proportion of the time.

Large building bricks are a great resource. A creative child may play alone with them for a while, merely calling for attention when the time comes to show what he has made. A less creative child often learns the possibilities by becoming involved in a joint activity with a parent or another child. Large empty detergent cartons can form good substitutes for commercially-produced blocks.

Water at the sink or in the bathroom holds the attention of most children. A mother, who was observed recently, presented several learning opportunities, very naturally, while she herself was busy cooking and her three-year-old hearing-impaired boy, Christopher, stood nearby on a chair at the sink. She explained that she had tried to interest him in her cooking, but that he had been really anxious to play at the sink and she saw no reason why he should not.

Christopher	*(Holding a plastic cup)* Mum!
Mother	*(Turning to look at Christopher)* What is it?
Christopher	Look! Water.
Mother	*(Pointing to a plastic jug)* See how many cups you can fill from that jug.
Christopher	*(Looking questioningly at mother)* Eh.
Mother	*(Pointing to the tap and to the jug)* Put some water in your jug and see how many cups it fills.
Christopher	*(Pours out a cupful and points to the water left in the jug.)* Water.
Mother	*(Pointing to two other cups)* That's right. Now pour that water into those other cups.
Christopher	*(Pointing to an empty cup)* That one?
Mother	*(As Christopher pours out without waiting)* Yes. That's right, and the other one.
Christopher	*(Drops the jug)* All fall down. Wet now.
Mother	*(Going over to the sink)* Oh dear, where's the cloth?
Christopher	*(Pointing to a red bucket)* Red one.
Mother	*(As Christopher brings the cloth)* I see. It's in the red bucket. Good boy. Wipe it all up now.

Christopher	*(Handing mother the jug)* Mummy go.
Mother	Oh, you want me to have a go. All right. Watch. *(Quickly pours out three cupfuls from the newly filled jug)* One, two, three.
Christopher	*(Clapping his hands)* Good Mummy!

One interesting feature of this particular interchange is the way in which the mother expected this little three-year-old boy, with a profound hearing loss, to follow instructions which might have stretched the capabilities of any three-year-old with normal hearing. When her demands puzzled him she gave a normal non-verbal accompaniment to her instruction as she pointed to both the tap and the jug. In context this was quite sufficient to convey her meaning. Another point of interest is the number of times that Christopher took the initiative. He was surprised to find water left in the jug and did not really know what to do with it. His utterance of, 'water' is really a request for advice. His mother fully understood this and gave another instruction which he checked before he obeyed. He was quick to act both verbally and practically, in response to his mother's question about the cloth. Following this, he took the initiative again as he organised his mother into having a go with the jug. He was delighted by her success and showed it. This transcript is an example of an interaction in which very big demands were made, but in such a way that there was no strain or fear of breakdown in communication. All too often hearing-impaired children are not challenged in this way and so they do not have the opportunity of working out, from a combination of verbal and contextual cues, what is expected of them.

Musical activities

Nursery rhymes sung over and over again, are often a great source of joy to hearing-impaired children who, in time, come to request their own favourites. Action rhymes, too, like 'Two little Dickie Birds' or 'This little Pig went to Market', can be fun.

Moving and dancing to music, of any kind, delights young children and hearing-impaired children are no exception in this respect. Making simple musical instruments and using them to keep time to music involves a wide use of language and develops listening skills. It is especially important to offer advice to parents of hearing-impaired children in this area because initially they may feel that the world of music is irrelevant to a child with a hearing loss. This is so far from the truth! Music can add another whole dimension to the world of the hearing-impaired child just as it can to that of a child with normal hearing.

Picture books and stories

Sharing books, especially at bedtime, can become a well-established routine and one to which most children look forward. In the case of hearing-impaired children, it may be wise for the professional offering guidance to the family to model a typical story session once or twice so that the right approach to story telling or the sharing of a book can be seen. In the author's experience, in this area particularly, there is need for help. The presence of the hearing loss seems to create a tendency for parents or other care-givers to use books as a means of labelling objects in the pictures, instead of as a basis for discussion of the central meaning that the illustrations carry.

Children enjoy becoming really familiar with a book so that they can anticipate what is on the next page. To have a little shelf of favourite books in the child's bedroom can be a valuable resource from which the child can choose a book which he would like as the basis of a bedtime story on any particular night. Practical advice of this nature is helpful to parents and is usually followed. It is often developed further once parents experience the enjoyment that comes from regularly sharing books in this way. Parents have such an intimate knowledge of their children, and of the experiences they have had together, that real sharing can take place as the pages of a book are turned.

As part of a guidance session, a parent and child are often happy to use a well-loved book to share with the professional. Lisa, aged four-and-a-half (with a hearing loss across the speech range of 90–95dB) arrived with her mother recently with three books in a bag. After taking off her coat Lisa took charge saying:

Lisa	*(Laying out the books)* Which one?
Professional	That one there please.
Lisa	*(Climbing on mother's knee)* Come on, Mum.
Mother	Now then, this is a story about a . . .
Lisa	'lock.
Mother	Yes, a very old clock, remember?
Lisa	Very old.
Mother	And the very old clock was in a very old house. And in the very old house there lived a . . . *(turning page and pointing)*
Lisa	Very old man.
Mother	That's right, look! There's the old man. He's very tired and he's fallen asleep.

And so together, Lisa and her mother 'told' this well-known story. It was quite obvious that this routine had developed over a long period of time and that both Lisa and her mother not only enjoyed it, but were also proud of their achievement and happy to share it with someone who had become a trusted friend.

Another valuable talking point can be a family photograph album.

Children really enjoy picking out people whom they know and trying to recall events related to them or talking about the actual events depicted in the photographs.

Outings

Outings can take so many forms. A walk down the street in the company of an interested adult can be a rich linguistic experience for a child. Any changes in the normal environment, or the activities of the people that they pass can all serve as talking points and as a basis for recollection or prediction.

The local park is usually a great scene of activity. Allowing the child to choose the areas of the park he wants to visit can give rise to a lot of discussion, as can chatter about the actual activities in which he engages once there.

Visits to relatives and friends can be anticipated and prepared for before they are undertaken. The journey, by car, bus or train, can provide many talking points as can the experiences shared with friends on arrival. The homeward journey may supply fresh experience or be a time to discuss what happened on the visit.

Holidays away from home provide a wealth of linguistic experiences if exploited to the full. Days and dates can be talked about and marked off on calendars as the holiday draws near. Suitcases and bags can be packed as a joint activity. If some choice is given in relation to the clothes and toys which are to be taken, there is often a lot to be discussed. With the help of pictures and photographs, plans can be made for what will be done on the holiday. Once the day of departure arrives, the journey itself, and later the time spent in the new environment, will provide one new experience after another about which to communicate. Photographs of the holiday provide a wonderful resource when memories are shared on the return home.

Special events like the visit of a circus to the town provide further opportunities to widen experience and serve as a good basis for real communication.

Sharing with other parents

Parents, once motivated and involved in the provision of a rich linguistic environment for their hearing-impaired child, are often very resourceful. It can be helpful to link up groups of parents who share the aim of helping their hearing-impaired children to achieve fluent spoken language. As they pool their experiences they have much to offer one another.

= 7 =
Language Through the Pre-school

> *It is one of the most important functions of the nursery school to ensure that children are supported in their acquisition of skills by the use of language which will provide them with coping strategies so necessary in later schooling which is almost entirely word based.*
>
> (Curtis, 1986)

These words were written in relation to a programme for children who have normal hearing. They take on an even greater significance when considered against the needs of hearing-impaired children whose early linguistic progress is likely to be slow on account of the reduced auditory cues they receive in communication situations.

It is significant that Curtis (1986) has identified, as a primary need, linguistic support for children as they acquire skills at the pre-school stage. Her words follow the results of recent investigations into the language environments of various pre-school settings. Wood *et al.* (1980) and Tizard and Hughes (1984) have produced evidence which throws doubt on previous assumptions about the linguistic climate of nursery schools and classes. For many years there was a commonly held belief that the staff of pre-school settings provided richer and more stimulating environments in which children, especially those from working class homes, had more opportunities to develop linguistically and educationally than they would have had at home. Tizard and Hughes found that both working class and middle class homes provided children with rich learning experiences of a different type from any they had found in the nursery provision. So strong was this evidence that, in the closing sentence of their book, they completely turn the tables on this issue as they stated:

> Indeed, in our opinion, it is time to shift the emphasis away from what parents should learn from professionals and towards what professionals can learn by studying parents and children at home.

In the light of such evidence parents and professionals who are considering pre-school placement for a hearing-impaired child, need to weigh matters up very carefully. If the home provides richer opportunities for language learning, through more one-to-one interaction with an adult who is closely attuned to the needs of the child, and who shares a common pool of experiences that allows for mutual understanding to develop, a very basic question must be faced in relation to children who have such great linguistic needs. Should nursery school or playgroup placement even be considered for young hearing-impaired children at the early stages of language development?

In the preceding chapters the need for good one-to-one interaction in the language learning process in the home has been highlighted. At the same time it has been emphasised that the needs of the hearing-impaired child should not dominate those of the family as a whole. Inevitably, however, in the process of meeting the special linguistic needs of the child, more individual attention than normal is often centred on that child. In order to maintain a balance in such a child's experience, therefore, it may be well to consider for at least part of the day, some form of pre-school placement where the child will be one of a group. Within it there will be opportunity for the child to interact with other children and with adults other than those of the immediate family. At all times it is necessary to keep a sense of proportion in relation to special needs and therefore, decisions about a hearing-impaired child must not be made on the grounds of linguistic need alone.

Selection of a pre-school placement

There are many factors to be considered by parents and professionals if pre-school placement is to be considered for a hearing-impaired child. The more carefully a placement is selected, the more benefit the child is likely to receive within it.

It must be remembered that the pre-school hearing-impaired child is learning to listen with the help of hearing-aids. It is necessary, therefore, right at the start, to determine what the acoustic conditions are in the proposed placement. Ross (1972) outlines the effects of background noise in classroom situations and a recent video-tape by Huntington (1986) brings this home in a very practical way. The use of a radio hearing-aid system should certainly be considered for hearing-impaired children who are to be placed in nursery school or playgroup situations.

Attention should also be given to the adult/child staffing ratio to ensure that the child's linguistic needs will be met adequately through frequent interaction with adults. The possibility should be explored of the provision of extra part-time staff to allow for daily one-to-one conversation sessions to be built into the programme. Bearing in mind that the probable linguistic level of the hearing-impaired child, at this stage, is comparable to that of a much younger child with normal hearing, it is obvious that this is an area of special need. There is a danger, however, in the use of the term 'special need' because it is sometimes interpreted as 'different need'. The hearing-impaired

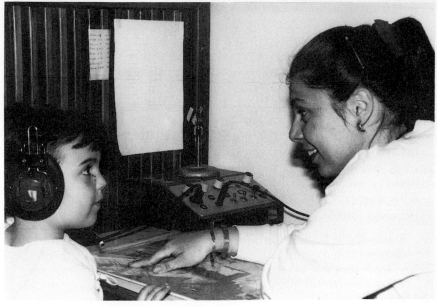

A four-year-old enjoying an individual chat about a picture

child's greatest need is, in fact, not for anything very *different* from that which the child with normal hearing has experienced earlier. It is for an extension of the period of one-to-one interaction, usually enjoyed by mother and child in the home, into whatever pre-school situation the hearing-impaired child may be placed.

A high adult/child ratio in a pre-school setting does not in itself ensure good adult/child interaction. The quality of the interaction is dependent on many factors. The formality or informality of the programme and the way in which language opportunities are exploited should be assessed. Certain issues must be addressed:

- Is it a teacher dominated programme providing little opportunity for children to experiment and explore?
- Is it such a free programme that children have 'experience' all the time, but little opportunity for interaction with adults and, therefore, little opportunity to learn from that experience?
- Does the programme cater for all aspects of the child's needs – intellectual, social, emotional, physical and aesthetic?
- What is the general linguistic level of the children in the programme? This is an important matter for consideration. In some British inner city areas so many children come from non-English speaking homes that the general linguistic competence, in English, of children with normal hearing is very limited. A hearing-impaired child from an English speaking home, or an ethnic

minority child to be educated in English may gain little linguistic motivation from placement in such a group.

- What proportion of the children have special needs? The balance between these children, with the demands that their special needs, of whatever nature, make on staff, and those who are not deemed to have special needs is a significant factor. Those seeking to provide an auditory oral way of life for hearing-impaired children make a definite decision, at this stage, *not* to place them in a special nursery, catering only for hearing-impaired children. They seek, instead, an environment in which the majority of children do not have specific special needs, so that a hearing-impaired child may have as much opportunity as possible to interact with children with normal language and behaviour. According to Webster and Ellwood (1985):

> Since deafness does not affect the child's biological capacity for learning language, if he is to use this capacity to the full, he needs more exposure to an ordinary speech environment and wide opportunities for play with peers already using language at his interest level.

- Will placement in the proposed pre-school programme serve as a good preparation for later compulsory schooling?

Unfortunately, in many areas of Britain today, there may be very little real choice of pre-school placement. Briault (1982), reviewing the situation, makes the point that the growth of pre-school provision since 1972 has been extremely uneven, it having been most rapid in inner city areas and least so in rural areas. It must be realised, therefore, that places for children with special needs may be hard to find due to pressure on existing services. Even when a suitable setting has been identified, it may not be possible to secure a place for a hearing-impaired child. As a result, it is possible that parents and professionals, assessing existing local pre-school provision, may well be unable to find the 'ideal' for a hearing-impaired child. They may, however, after careful consideration of all the factors concerned, find a placement which it is felt would widen the hearing-impaired child's experience.

It must always be remembered that any such placement should be looked upon as an addition to what the home can offer. Margaret McMillan (1919), a pioneer of nursery school education, was one of the first educators to realise the important part that parents could play in the education of their children. She laid down, as a basic principle, that nursery school provision should be viewed as *an extension of*, and not *a substitute for* the home. Those responsible for the placement of a hearing-impaired child in a pre-school setting need to weigh up the complementary contributions of home and school in every case, and to strike a balance in respect of the proportion of time that the child might spend in the pre-school setting. The needs of every hearing-impaired child are different, as are the circumstances of their families, and it is therefore not possible to lay down hard and fast rules about the degree of involvement that there should be in pre-school programmes. Where local provision has allowed, the author's experience has been that many hearing-impaired children have benefited initially from short spells in the placement, for example, two half days per week. In time, they have adjusted well to these periods being lengthened gradually until they have reached five half days per week. Such an arrangement ensures that there is sufficient time at home for interaction with the mother and other members of the family, as well as allowing the child to have the wider experience of placement in a group of children.

Preparation for pre-school placement

Preparation of the staff

The professional who has offered guidance to the family since diagnosis is probably the person who will help them to find a suitable pre-school placement. It will also be the responsibility of the professional to train the staff within that setting. The needs of the staff will vary according to their previous experience, or lack of it, with hearing-impaired children. Time spent on this issue, prior to the admission of the child with special needs, can have very positive results.

The effects of a hearing loss on a young child's developing language need to be explained, and realistic expectations of what can be achieved must be outlined. The showing of a longitudinal video-tape of an older child, with a hearing loss similar to the child to be admitted to the programme, may serve a very useful purpose at this stage. To see a child at the very early stages of learning to listen and to communicate, and then to follow through the many stages to fluent oral communication can illustrate, as nothing else can, just what the future may hold for the child in question. It may also show what part those involved with the child in the early years can play.

Such a video-tape can serve a double purpose. In addition to setting realistic expectations, it can illustrate the type of interaction that is possible for adult and child to enjoy. The professional can use it as a basis for pointing out the significant features of that interaction, for example, the use of normal, natural language by the adult, arising out of something that is of real interest to the child; the responsiveness of the adult to any contribution that the child makes, be it verbal or non-verbal; and above all, it is necessary to point out that what can be seen is not an attempt merely to increase a child's vocabulary but is rather the effort of both adult and child to share meaning.

Yet another purpose served by the showing of an appropriate video-tape is the opportunity it provides for the professional to point out what things are *not* happening! It is important to highlight the absence of exaggerated mouth movements, the lack of emphasis on single words, the fact that there are not continual requests from the adult for the child to repeat words correctly. It also provides the opportunity to discuss the fact that no manual system of any kind is in use. Staff may have had preconceived ideas about the special needs of 'deaf' children and may have thought it proper to use signs or to learn sign language in order to prepare for the reception of the child. At the same time, a professional advocating an auditory oral way of life for a hearing-impaired child, should explain that natural gestures must be accepted from the child as he seeks to convey ideas for which he does not yet have spoken language. In such a situation the staff must be advised to use the spoken language that the child lacks, in context. It must also be made clear that they should feel free to use all the normal non-verbal cues which occur in everyday communication situations, for example, facial expressions, head and hand movements.

Ways in which staff can help to meet the hearing-impaired child's special linguistic needs should be discussed in a very positive way. An outline of how the daily programme might be adapted to allow for more one-to-one interaction with the child is usually welcomed, as are suggestions for adult involvement, of the right kind, in play situations.

The fact that a hearing-impaired child is not a child who *cannot hear* but, rather, one who *is learning to listen* must be put across very forcibly. Time must be taken to demonstrate the power of a hearing-aid to help the child. Once again video-tapes can be used to illustrate this. If an older child with a hearing loss, similar to that of the child to be admitted to the programme, can be observed having a speech audiogram taken, with and without hearing-aids, a comparison of the scores of the two tests usually makes this point well, and helps to develop very positive attitudes towards the use of hearing-aids. The limitations of the hearing-aids must be explained as well as the importance of considering the child's physical position in class. The effect of distance from the microphone on the signal that the child receives through the hearing-aids must be understood and the advantage and use of some form of radio hearing-aid system should be discussed and demonstrated.

Day-to-day maintenance of the hearing-aids must be dealt with carefully. It is helpful if responsibility for this area is delegated to one or two specific members of staff. Spare parts for the hearing-aids should be left on site as should, wherever possible, complete spare hearing-aids of the same type. If this is not possible, information about how to acquire replacement aids when required must be available.

Earmoulds should be discussed – their cleanliness and their fit. The staff must know that feedback from an earmould should be reported to the specialist teacher immediately. They must be aware that turning down the volume is no solution to the problem and that it does, in fact, detract from the value of the aid to the child. Staff must be aware of the recommended setting for the child's hearing-aids and should contact the visiting specialist immediately if, for any reason the child is not happy to wear the aids at the correct settings. In addition there should be a clearly defined procedure to follow in the case of lost or broken earmoulds.

The possibility of a variable hearing loss at a time when a hearing-impaired child has a cold or other middle ear problem should be mentioned. If staff suspect such a condition they should know whom to contact and should arrange for medical help to be available if the parent has not already done so.

The everyday management of the child is an important area to be considered. It should be made quite clear that normal standards of behaviour can be expected from a hearing-impaired child. Staff should be warned against making one concession after another on account of hearing loss. At the same time, they need to be alerted to situations in which the child may misunderstand or not hear instructions at all.

The full involvement of the hearing-impaired child in the programme should be discussed. Some members of staff may be surprised that a child with a hearing loss should be given the opportunity to take part in musical activities. Without appropriate advice they may plan to exclude the child from this part of the programme. Others feel that story time is not helpful to a child with very limited language. They need positive help to come to an understanding of how a hearing-impaired child can gain so much from such an experience if properly handled. Video-tape extracts of other hearing-impaired children involved in such situations offer reassurance on these and similar matters.

During the initial period of preparation it is important that the professional involved in staff training conveys the positive attributes of the hearing-impaired child. Time must be set aside to emphasise everything that the child can do. It should be pointed out that the child is first a child and second a hearing-impaired child. The experiences which promote good all-round development in children with normal hearing are those, therefore, that will best meet the general needs, and probably if handled well, also the special needs of the hearing-impaired child.

Above all, the staff of the proposed placement must have the assurance that if the hearing-impaired child is admitted, they will have regular contact with a specialist professional who will visit regularly and answer questions as they arise. They must also be confident that they will receive help from the specialist in assessing whether or not the child's special needs are being adequately met in their environment.

Preparation of the children already in the programme

There are two distinct schools of thought on this point in relation to nursery-aged children. One holds that young pre-school children are too wrapped up in their own worlds to be concerned about another child wearing hearing-aids, and proposes that questions should be answered only if and when they arise. The other believes that it is advisable to prepare the ground for the admission of the hearing-impaired child, at least to a limited extent. Games involving the senses, talk about spectacles and 'play' with a hearing-aid to discover what it does, have all been used to this end. The author has had wide experience of children placed in settings holding these differing views, but has seen no significant differences in the way in which the hearing-impaired children have been accepted within them. As is the case with any child, the main factors determining acceptance seem to be the child's basic personality and degree of social maturity.

Preparation of the parents

Prior to the placement of the child in a pre-school setting there should be ample opportunity for the parents to attend with the child for short spells. This allows the staff who will be dealing with the child to become known and the daily routine to become familiar. Parents need to be reassured by the staff that they are happy to accept a hearing-impaired child and that they do not anticipate any great problems because of the hearing loss. They also need to feel sure that the staff will consult them if any problems do arise, and to know that the staff will expect them to share any worries that they may have about the child with them.

The importance of keeping a regular home/school book should be explained to parents, and a drawing book issued for this purpose. Schools should set the pattern by daily entries of items of interest that have occurred there and should expect parents to reciprocate with accounts of events at home. Simple pictures with short sentences are all that are needed to keep a good home/school link. Some adults are very self-conscious about their own attempts to draw and parents need to be assured that anything that they can offer can be used as a basis for conversation with their child. It is also important for the parent to be encouraged to discuss with the child any entries in the book made by the staff.

Preparation of the child

Any pre-placement visits have very real significance for the hearing-impaired child, as well as for the parent. As the child becomes familiar with the setting, he comes to feel secure and to develop confidence within it, and anticipation of future visits can be fostered. Photographs taken during a visit, showing the children, members of staff, and equipment, form good talking points at home, especially with members of the family who have not seen the place. If these are talked about on a child's return from a visit and, again, as another visit is due, they prepare the child for attendance.

The more independent a child is, the more happily he is likely to settle in a group without the mother. Parents should, therefore, be encouraged to do as much as possible to ensure that the child can attend to his own physical needs. It is important to make sure that he knows what to do if he requires help. There is a tendency for parents to over-protect a child with a handicap and to do too much for him. Sometimes parents are very sensitive when this issue is raised by a professional. The possible future placement of the child in a pre-school setting provides a fresh opportunity for this subject to be raised, and can motivate the parent to work towards helping the child to greater independence.

In addition to contact with the actual proposed placement, it can be helpful if parents are advised, prior to the child's admission, to arrange for the child to mix with a few neighbourhood children for short spells. It is ideal if any of these children happen to attend the nursery school or playgroup to which the child will go but, even if not, a little informal contact with other children, near home, can serve as good preparation.

Experience in the pre-school setting

In the small setting of the home the hearing-impaired child will have been very much the centre of attention. That world changes when the child is placed in a group of children who have to share the attention of a few adults. Behaviour that has been acceptable within the family may not be acceptable within the larger group. For the child to discover this can, initially, be a very strange experience. Gradually he must learn how to socialise with the other children in the group and how, also, to interact with the adults in this new environment.

It is very important that the pre-school setting should be a welcoming place for little children. Whatever the adult/child ratio, resources are well-deployed if one or two adults are specifically designated the task of welcoming the children on arrival and of chatting with them as they are helped off with coats etc. The time of arrival is often the moment when a child really has something to tell and is highly motivated to share it with a friendly adult.

Recently, the author observed the arrival of children at a nursery

Arrival at pre-school is the time to share news with a friend

into which a few hearing-impaired children integrate well. A special feature of this particular programme is the welcome afforded the children on arrival. The adult/child ratio is not high and so, in order to ensure that ample time is available to give each child an adequate welcome, the domestic staff have been recruited into this part of the programme before they start the chores of the day. This has proved to have far reaching effects. The domestic staff now take more interest in the children than before and provide them with lots of incidental conversational opportunities throughout the day. One child after another, both hearing and hearing-impaired alike, could be seen running to an adult on arrival and initiating conversation about some item of clothing or about something proudly produced from a schoolbag. The children so obviously felt that they had come into a place where the adults were genuinely interested in them and in what they had been doing or had brought to show.

Even these adults, however, cannot know as much about each child as do the members of that child's family. They cannot have the rich store of shared experience built up over the years by mother and child. This is drawn upon, often quite unconsciously, as parent and child communicate in the home. It must be remembered that for the child new to a pre-school setting, the common basis of shared experience which has supported that child's communication hitherto, is now lacking. Garvey (1984) reminds us of this when she says 'Conversations thrive in familiar settings and with familiar persons.'

In spite of a warm welcome by a friendly adult a new child may be reluctant to express himself in any way or to join a group of children. The hesitant child should be shown what activities are on offer and given time to observe from the sidelines without being pressurised into a group. Some tentative approach is usually made to a group once the child feels confident enough to become involved.

Too much can be attributed to the presence of a hearing loss. It must always be remembered that any group of young children is made up of little individuals, whether hearing or hearing impaired, each with a distinctive personality. The features of this personality often have more effect on a child's inclination to mix well or quickly with other children than does the presence of a hearing loss. A naturally relaxed, gregarious child will settle more quickly into group activities than a tense or diffident child.

Much is learned about the meaning and purpose of language as children interact with each other in group situations. Thus, a hearing-impaired child's motivation to master the skill of talking may develop rapidly as he learns to assert his rights and share his ideas with his peers in a group. It must never be forgotten, however, that it is unusual for a child, still at the very early stages of acquiring fluency in his mother tongue, to be placed regularly in a group situation. Most children when at this stage are still with mother in the home. Unless adequate provision is made to provide the child, whose language skills are very limited, with regular opportunities for one-to-one interaction with an adult, language may not develop and the child may become a passive observer of the group.

Much of the child's time will be spent in play in whatever pre-school setting he is placed. Wherever there is a group of children the layout of play areas is important. There should be plenty of choice in order to cater for a wide range of needs and interests. Areas for boisterous physical play should be included, as should a house corner, scope for imaginative play, a quiet corner for table activities, a book corner with comfortable seating, a 'messy' area with sand, water, paint and clay, a building area and space to move around in and to adapt according to passing needs, for example, one week it may serve as a hospital and on another week it may be used for a hairdresser's shop.

While children are at play, different kinds of adult involvement are displayed by staff in different pre-school settings. There are those who feel that to interact with children at play is to intrude and, in fact, a certain kind of involvement can indeed become an intrusion. Wood *et al.* (1980) found that when staff became involved in the children's play or constructive activities, and tried to converse with the children, the situation tended to become adult dominated and to turn into a question and answer session. Curtis (1986), however, identifies support through the use of language, as one of the most important functions of the nursery school. Her wording is highly significant. She does not talk about the function as being that of 'teaching language', but suggests that it is as the children are acquiring skills that language has to be used. Many of these skills are acquired through play and, therefore, there is an obvious need for adults to develop the ability to interact with children as they play in such a way that they do not dominate the situation.

What is needed in the wider sphere of the pre-school setting is a continuation of the type of exposure to language that the child has had in the home with the mother, where talk has centred round the child's activities of the moment. This is particularly important for hearing-impaired children whose linguistic skills are less well developed than those of their hearing peers. As they explore and exploit the challenges of the pre-school setting, adults should be at hand to chat with them about their activities, not in a domineering way, but in a manner which involves them as partners in the interaction. These adults must be good listeners as they try to tune in to the young child's imperfect attempts to share meaning. A child's progress at this stage is very tied to the style of interaction adopted by the adults in the environment. Wood *et al.* (1980) state:

> The way in which a child makes use of an adult as a talking resource depends very largely upon the way that the adult presents herself to him in conversation.

The whole of a pre-school session is not taken up with play. Through its varied programme the child is presented with a new range of linguistic experiences. The everyday routine necessary for the management of a group of young children provides ample opportunity for the repetition of language in meaningful contexts and, although it may not do much to encourage the development of the child's expressive language skills, it can be a real confidence builder. As the hearing-impaired child is faced, time and time again, with the same requests in the same situations, for example, 'Now wash your hands' or 'Please put these toys away', understanding develops and confidence grows as the child experiences success.

Most children enjoy group storytime and, provided that the period set aside for this activity is fairly short, there is no reason why a hearing-impaired child should not form part of the group for a story with the teacher using well-illustrated material which will help to carry something of the central meaning of the story. Much can be gained if time can be set aside after a group storytime, to share the story again with that child on a one-to-one basis. If well-handled, such a situation provides the child with the opportunity to use language across a wide range of functions – to explain, to reason, to predict, to project or to imagine.

Music usually has a regular slot in any pre-school programme and young children love to move to music, to make music and to sing. As mentioned previously, hearing-impaired children are no exception in this respect and in fact, for some, musical activities play a very significant part in the development of their communication skills. Such activities appear, on occasion, to be the means of first opening up the world of sound to a hearing-impaired child. Not only is this true of the reception of sound but also of its production. Taite (1986) studied a group of hearing-impaired children attending a special nursery school department. She reported that there was a measurable increase in the number of vocalisations made by a group of pre-school children when they were singing. The natural repetition that so many songs provide means that, within a thoroughly enjoyable activity, children have the opportunity to hear the same phrases over and over again.

Conclusion

Each pre-school programme is unique, but all have much in common. Staff in each situation decide what proportion of time is allocated for free play and what proportion involves children in directed activities. Whatever the general framework of the programme, those working within it must remember that, however the activities occur, there are many times during the day when children will benefit from sharing them with an adult who can provide the language to accompany the activity, and so, too, help the children to verbalise the experience that they are enjoying. Tamburrini (1982) lays down wise guidelines:

> Nursery teachers need to do more than provide a rich range of materials with which children generate and direct their activities. They need also to adopt a role which includes interacting with children in a way that synchronizes with their intentions and purposes.

= 8 =
Language Through Entry to Primary School

> When we make laws that compel our children to go to school we assume collectively an awesome responsibility.
>
> (Donaldson, 1978)

With the above words Donaldson brings home the weight of responsibility that rests on the shoulders of educators. She is not advocating de-schooling, but is challenging those responsible for planning the school experience to ensure that it is as good as it can be made.

Age of entry

The age of entry to school varies from country to country. In Britain itself there are regional variations. Some local educational authorities admit children to primary school at the beginning of the school year in which they are five. This can mean that the youngest child in a group may be only just four years of age. Other local educational authorities adopt the policy of admitting children at the beginning of the term in which they will turn five. A Government publication related to 'Achievement in Primary Schools' (HMSO, 1986) recommends that:

> Local education authorities should, if they do not already do so, and under suitable conditions, move towards allowing entry into the maintained education system at the beginning of the school year in which the child becomes five.

Concern was expressed in the Report, however, about the unplanned way in which the admission of children has grown up. It was felt that, as a result, the educational needs of the youngest children were not being adequately met. The suggestion is made that for these young children the most suitable conditions are likely to be found in nursery classes where part-time attendance is possible for those under the age of five years.

Bearing in mind the probable linguistic retardation of a hearing-impaired child at the four-to-five-year-old level, it can be seen that the age of admission to primary school for such a child is worthy of very serious consideration. In the author's experience, the vast majority of children with severe and profound hearing losses need 'nursery school type' education between the ages of four and five years. Those responsible for educational placement must ensure that, if there is to be early placement in a primary school, hearing-impaired children do not have *their* special linguistic needs sacrificed because of the attention that must be given to the older children in the group in relation to the development of their literacy and mathematical skills.

The educational placement

The placement of a hearing-impaired child of compulsory school age involves the consideration of more factors than that of a child with normal hearing. The Education Act, 1981 (in Britain) has shifted the emphasis from the category of handicap to that of the special educational needs of any particular child. Its recommendation that, wherever possible, a child with special educational needs should be educated in the ordinary school, is very much in line with the thinking that has motivated those working with hearing-impaired children who, over the years have pioneered the principle of integration. In this respect the field of 'deaf education' has led the way. For many years now, the majority of pre-school and large numbers of school-aged children have been placed into classes of those with normal hearing.

The Education Act (1981) lays down certain conditions that serve as sound guidelines if efficiently followed. When the placement of a handicapped child is under consideration, certain criteria should be met. There should be, within the proposed setting, sufficient help and equipment available to meet the child's special needs. At the same time, the Act makes it clear that the rights of children without special needs are safeguarded. It lays down that the placement of a child with special needs in an ordinary school should be compatible with, 'the provision of efficient education for the children with whom he will be educated.' A third condition relates to the efficient use of resources.

Another positive feature of the Act is the provision for an annual review of each child's special educational needs and of the way in which these are being met in the present placement. This allows for change, where necessary, and so initial placement at infant school stage (five- to seven-year-olds) is not necessarily one for the child's whole school life.

In the case of hearing-impaired children, however, it is very important that those who are involved in judging the progress that these children are making, have enough knowledge to know what constitutes progress. If those with little experience of what hearing-impaired children can achieve and little understanding of how it is achieved are allocated the task of making assessments, there are times when too little, and other times when too much is expected of a hearing-impaired child. The author, from experience, can cite several instances of pressure being brought to bear on parents and teachers to have a young child removed from the programme because that child's initial progress seemed so slow that it was feared, by professionals with insufficient experience of the approach, that the child would never talk. This pressure was resisted and these very children are now young people with fluent oral communication skills and a degree of confidence that allows them to mix freely in hearing society. The real problem is that, to date, there is no satisfactory test of developing conversational competence. Many of the tests administered to hearing-impaired children at the early stages highlight only what they *cannot* do and miss the positive elements of communicative competence which are developing and that are a firm foundation for normal linguistic progress. The most satisfactory way to illustrate such features is, undoubtedly, by longitudinal video-taped records, taken at regular intervals. These show the individual linguistic progress that a child has made over a period of months. This may be difficult to describe, and it may not affect the score of a standardised test, but it will be clearly visible on an extract of video-tape as the child's interaction with a member of staff is examined.

In most local education authorities, teachers, medical officers, psychologists and parents are involved in identifying the extent of a child's special educational needs and, consequently, in making a recommendation about the setting in which those needs might most effectively be met. In the case of a hearing-impaired child, the type of special educational provision that is required may be the subject of considerable debate. It will be obvious that the child's special needs usually arise from lack of linguistic competence due to the hearing loss. The way in which these special linguistic needs are to be met is an area in which professionals may have differing views. Those who are concerned that the hearing-impaired child should enjoy an auditory oral way of life, with the opportunity to develop conventional communicative competence, require the environment to be as normal as possible. It should be one in which the importance of good interaction between adults and children is fully appreciated, and also one in which there is ample provision for such children to 'make an important contribution to developing their own linguistic skills' (Webster and Ellwood, 1985).

Under the terms of the Education Act (1981) there is more provision than ever before for parents to have a say in the type of educational setting in which they want their child to be placed. If, as has been suggested in an earlier chapter of this book, parents have had the opportunity to visit a variety of provision, they will be in a position to make an informed decision regarding the suitability of any placement recommended by a local education authority for their child. On the surface there appear to be three options:

1   An ordinary school (with some extra support for the hearing-impaired child).
2   A special unit attached to an ordinary school (allowing for varying degrees of integration).
3   A special school.

The situation, however, is much more complicated than it appears. The method of communication used with hearing-impaired children within these settings varies from area to area.

The ordinary school

In most ordinary schools a hearing-impaired child will be surrounded by only normal, natural language and should have support from a specialist teacher for the hearing impaired. The main problem in this situation, for those dealing with a five-year-old with a severe to profound hearing loss, is to ensure that there is adequate support. In addition to all the exposure that the child will have to the curriculum devised for children with normal hearing, sufficient opportunity must be afforded the hearing-impaired child to be active in the development of his oral communication skills. Those placing a five-year-old hearing-impaired child with very limited linguistic ability into a group of ordinary children with well-developed oral language, must assess carefully the extent of the individual support needed to allow that child ample opportunity to practise the skill of talking.

A special unit within an ordinary school

There is great variety in the type of support a hearing-impaired child may have in a special unit attached to an ordinary school. Some units act as a base from which children go out to spend most of their time in classes for children with normal hearing, but to which they return to receive whatever degree of individual support they need. Other units operate almost like a small special school – physically near the classes for ordinary children, but offering only very limited degrees of integration into them. Some units provide a rich, normal linguistic environment, ensuring that their hearing-impaired children are exposed to nothing but normal, natural language at a normal rate of utterance. Others use structured language schemes and some are supporting their oral communication with one of the sign systems. It is, therefore, very necessary for those anxious for a hearing-impaired child to have a wholly auditory oral way of life, to ensure that, if a unit placement is under consideration, the particular unit into which the child will go is one in which normal, natural language is used at all

A group hearing-aid allows children to share each other's contributions

times and one in which there is no form of manual back-up.

Decisions need to be made on the basis of individual need about the amount of time any particular hearing-impaired child will spend in an integrated situation. The linguistic level of the child will be the main determining factor in this issue. Timetables and staffing levels must take into consideration the individual needs of the children in relation to having sufficient opportunity to develop good oral communication skills through interaction on a one-to-one basis.

A special school

Unfortunately, because of the low level of spoken language achieved by many who were educated in the old traditional schools for the deaf, the term 'special school' in relation to hearing-impaired children has become almost synonymous with an educational environment in which there is a heavy weight of manual communication. This can be very misleading. Several special schools, in Britain and elsewhere do, in fact, provide a rich language enabling environment within which children with severe and profound hearing losses (many of whom have additional handicaps) come through to a level of spoken language that allows them to take their places in society at large. In these schools no sign system is in use and the children use spoken language as their means of communication both outside and inside the classroom. It is reassuring and refreshing to have this point recognised by independent observers. Lynas *et al.* (1988) say:

There are several oral schools in this country with high reputations and good records of academic achievement and oral language.

There can be no rule of thumb guidelines laid down regarding the educational placement of hearing-impaired children because the needs of each child are different, but one thing must be made clear: the recommendation for placement should be made in the light of each child's specific needs and not in the light of what local provision already exists. There should be a range of provision available in every area. The author is, at the time of writing, involved with a developing programme for hearing-impaired children in Turkey and it has much to offer. It is a centre for hearing-impaired children situated next to an ordinary primary school and junior high school. It runs its own pre-school service including a nursery school for children with normal hearing into which the hearing-impaired children can integrate. On the recommendation of professionals, taking into account the wishes of parents, there is on offer one of the following options to severely and profoundly hearing-impaired children:

1   Full-time integration in one of the classes for normally hearing children with support from a specialist teacher of the hearing impaired of at least one hour per day.
2   A combination of part-time integration in the classes of the ordinary school with part-time education in the Centre, according to individual need.
3   Full-time education in the Centre but with opportunity for social integration with the children from the ordinary schools.

The flexibility of such a system has much to recommend it.

In whatever situation a hearing-impaired child is placed, a priority must be to ensure that there is sufficient support of the right kind to allow for interaction with an adult in a one-to-one situation, on a daily basis, until such time as the child has developed a degree of linguistic fluency that makes for linguistic independence. For some young children with severe or profound hearing losses this can involve two or three individual sessions per day. Only if such provision is made will children have the opportunity to practise putting their thoughts and ideas into words with adults who will listen attentively to what they are trying to say, and who are able to accept and expand their offerings. This is very demanding on the resources of a class of ordinary children or on those of a unit where there is a group of children with a very wide range of special needs. If intensive help on a one-to-one basis is required, then placement in a special school which concentrates on the provision of a rich language learning environment, and in which fluent oral communication skills develop, may well be the best placement for the hearing-impaired child.

It becomes clear that an auditory oral way of life for hearing-impaired children may exist within any of the three options available – an ordinary school, a unit attached to an ordinary school, or a special school. As Wood (1982) points out, it is not so much the type of placement that matters as what goes on between the child, his peers, and the adults within it.

The transition from pre-school to school

One of the main differences between informal pre-school education and that of programmes for children once compulsory school age is reached, is the more systematic nature of the latter. At the pre-school stage adults are, as it were, standing on the side-lines, ready to intervene as and when appropriate. Brown (1980) refers to the type of support that adults offer at this stage as an attempt to 'add a pebble to the pile'. The fact that interaction of this nature follows the immediate interests and activities of the children makes it very meaningful to them. At the same time, it places a restraint on the adult insofar as it cannot really be pre-planned or, necessarily sustained, because the interest on which it is based can be random and, at times, very fleeting. The skill of those working in the infant school is to be able to marry the process of making opportunities for systematic learning with that of exploiting to the full the age-appropriate interests of the children. The perspective in which Lock (1980) views the learning of a child may be helpful here. He sees the child, not as someone responsible for developing strategies for the acquisition of knowledge on his own, but as one to whom these strategies are transmitted through his interactions with those who are already in possession of them. Lock calls the process one of 'guided reinvention'.

In the old days in Britain, and still today in many other countries, entrance to compulsory schooling was synchronous with a complete break with the child-centred learning that the pre-school years had fostered. It was held that, if learning experiences were to be widened and organised, a pre-arranged body of knowledge must be systematically planned by teachers and imparted to children. This led to teacher dominated classrooms in which there was little opportunity for children to have any interaction with either teacher or peer group. Such an environment is particularly inappropriate for hearing-impaired children who, on account of their hearing loss come into school with very limited oral communication skills.

Wells (1986) warns against formality of this nature even for children who have normal hearing. He feels that there should not be 'a sharp break with the incidental style of learning experienced at home'. He goes on to suggest that teachers should take as their basis and seek to extend 'the strategies that children have developed for actively making sense of experience'. He states his case forcibly as he claims that children's strategies should not be suppressed 'by the imposition of learning tasks for which they can see neither a purpose nor a connection with what they already know and can do'.

Principles of programming to meet linguistic needs

This section does not set out to describe any particular method of teaching nor to deal in detail with the approach to subjects of the curriculum. It is concerned with the basic principles underlying the planning and operation of a programme that will provide opportunities for children to continue the process of learning language through living in the school environment, as they have done formerly in the pre-school. It deals only with the development of spoken language because the author sees this as basic to all future progress in reading and writing, and therefore to the work of the curriculum as a whole. Tough (1977) claims that:

> The skills that are developed through experiences of participating in dialogue are those skills of thinking and using language that would seem to provide the very basis from which education can proceed.

Bruce (1987), after reviewing the work of pioneers in the field of early childhood education in general, lays down as one important principle that what children can do should be the starting point in a child's education. A primary need of any teacher faced with the task of educating a hearing-impaired child, is to find out at what level that child is functioning. Whoever has been dealing with the child prior to the age of compulsory schooling must share, with those to be responsible for that child at school age, in such a way that the fullest possible picture is painted of the child's strengths and weaknesses. Only by doing this can educators hope to meet the child's special educational needs. In this respect it is very important that those who receive a five-year-old hearing-impaired child should be made aware of all that he *can* do, because often all that is obvious at surface level by this age is how much he *cannot* do in relation to his hearing peers.

Once the child is in the programme, time must be set aside to observe him carefully in order to discover what learning strategies he has developed. Early on, staff must come to an understanding of the child's linguistic level and of the experiences that have brought him to it.

It must never be forgotten, however, that a hearing-impaired child is first and foremost a child, and then a child with a hearing loss and resultant language delay. Hearing-impaired children at the five- to seven-year-old level are, therefore, likely to benefit most of all from all the activities planned for their hearing peers. There is always the danger that if too much stress is laid on a child's special linguistic needs, teachers will feel that speech and language work of a very different nature must be specially planned, and they may set out to teach the hearing-impaired child lists of vocabulary and specific aspects of syntax. Teachers must be brought to the realisation that a classroom in which a normal curriculum is followed is the best educational setting for a hearing-impaired child. This 'normal' programme may operate in an ordinary school, a unit or in a special school that follows a normal curriculum.

Hearing impaired, like ordinary children, are greatly helped if they enter a well-organised programme. If the school day follows a regular routine so that, on the whole, children can predict what will happen next, they come to an understanding of instructions as they learn to associate them with the activity to which they relate, just as they will have done in the home in the early mother/child routines. A sense of security is fostered by the knowledge of what is likely to happen next and this brings with it a confidence which is essential if a child is to relax and learn.

There needs to be a sense of balance to a programme too. Part of the day should be devoted to group activities but, for hearing-impaired children especially, there must be daily opportunity for conversation with an adult on a one-to-one basis. Part of the time planned for the groups should be devoted to an educational play session within which the children have ample opportunity to experiment and explore and to have social interaction with their hearing peers. The rest of the time allocated for group activities may be more teacher directed, often involving some topic of general interest or the enjoyment of sharing a story.

Variety of subject matter is another component of a well-balanced programme. All subjects of the curriculum should be included – music, physical education, art and craft can all be interwoven with conversation, reading, scientific and mathematical work. Nor must the informal opportunities be neglected. Some of the richest language arises at 'clearing up' times or at times of preparation for the next activity.

Teacher style

Good organisation alone will not ensure a rich language learning situation. According to Wells and Nicholls (1985):

> The quality of pupil learning is strongly affected by the quality of interaction through which that learning is mediated.

This leads on to the need to look at teachers' styles. Wood (1986) and his colleagues have looked in depth at the effects of very different styles of teacher conversation on the same children and have discovered that:

> Too much control stifles the child, but too little robs the teacher of opportunities to help the child discover how to make himself understood.

The challenge for the teacher is to strike the right balance in interaction with hearing-impaired children, not only in one-to-one, but also in group situations. On the whole teachers talk too much and give children too little opportunity to make their contribution to a conversation or discussion. Teachers ask too many questions and do not give the children enough time to answer them. Teachers often have a preconceived idea of the way in which a conversation should go and so do not really listen to what it is the children are trying to say. They need to become better *listeners* so that in their interactions with the children they will pick up what it is that a child wants to express and in this way meaning really will be shared. Different classroom situations call for different styles, but the teacher who is anxious to provide opportunities for children to develop their linguistic skills will, on the whole, adopt a collaborative rather than a didactic style. Young children seem to have a natural urge to learn, and a collaborative style on the part of a teacher does much to foster and sustain this drive to find out more. As teacher and child explore ideas together, either in group or in individual situations, opportunities arise for the teacher to catch the moments when children are most willing and able to learn.

Such a teaching style can also be the means of helping a child to take responsibility for his own learning as he gradually develops his thinking skills. The characteristics of a good thinker have been outlined by a group of experienced educators under the leadership of Brierley (1969). They constitute a formidable list: confidence, concentration, the ability to estimate, the ability to synthesize and to seek analysis, the power to imagine, and to communicate in language. A situation in which teacher and child relate to each other as partners, is one in which these characteristics have the chance to develop. If hearing-impaired children are to become independent learners a collaborative approach is essential. It provides the teacher with an insight into the process by which the child is learning – into both his strengths and weaknesses – in a way that no other approach can do. It is interesting that Her Majesty's Inspectors, in a recent publication on Primary Schools (1987) identify some aspects of good practice and highlight the importance of an informality in the classroom which allows for discussion and nurtures a sense of self-discipline.

Some of the theoretical points made in this chapter can best be illustrated by studying a few abstracts of interactions recorded by the author when she had the opportunity to spend a morning observing a primary school class of thirty-four five- to seven-year-olds, vertically grouped. Two of the children had very severe hearing losses (both over 90dB across the speech range). This class had one full-time teacher, not specially trained for hearing-impaired children, one full-time classroom assistant, and additional help for the first hour and a half of each day from another teacher who had trained normal nursery school work.

The morning began with a session of educational play in a large playroom which had been well set out prior to the children's arrival at school. Children came into this playroom direct from the cloakroom where they had changed shoes etc. One teacher was in the cloakroom meeting the children and the other was in the playroom as was the classroom assistant. It is impossible to record all that happened during the play session, but even a few transcripts serve to illustrate the collaborative styles of the adults involved.

Transcript 1 – At the fun boat

Quite early on in the session one of the teachers was called on by a little girl asserting her right to have first turn on a fun boat.

Child	Miss _____ it should be me first.
Teacher	Why?
Child	I want first go.
Teacher	Didn't you have first go yesterday?
Child	Ye–es.
Teacher	Well, I'd let Alan have his turn now and then you can go next. That would be fair, wouldn't it?
Child	All right then. I'll wait.

Here the teacher's willingness to listen to the child's claim, and the friendly way in which she talked the matter through with the child, ensured that the little girl was led to do the socially acceptable thing and to feel that she had chosen to do so.

Transcript 2 – In the wendy house

One of the hearing-impaired children was playing in this group. She was acting as the mother.

Child 1	We're having a party.
Teacher	Is it a Christmas party?
Child 2	*(Acting as father)* No, it's a birthday party.
Hearing-impaired child	*(Offering a plate)* Here you are – birthday.
Teacher	Thank you. I love birthday cake.
Hearing-impaired child	Tea.

Teacher	Oh, thank you. I do love a cup of tea. Whose birthday is it?
Child 2	*(Pointing to Child 1)* It's his birthday. He's eight.
Teacher	Is it really your birthday today?
Child 1	No, just pretend. I'll be in the other school when I'm eight.
Teacher	Thanks for the tea. I must be going.
Hearing-impaired child	Bye bye.
Teacher	Bye.

This was a piece of cooperative dramatic play. The children had accepted roles and were acting accordingly. The teacher's invited intervention called for answers to relevant questions. The month was December and so it could have been a Christmas party. Her statements also evoked responses. Her checking of the validity of the birthday shared with the children that she understood that this was just a make believe situation. The quick response of the hearing-impaired child to the teacher's announcement that she was about to leave, shows that this little girl was thoroughly involved and fully aware of what was happening, although her expressive language was much more limited than that of her hearing friends. It was nevertheless appropriate for the occasion.

Transcript 3 – In the Lego corner

The classroom assistant had sat down at a table where one little boy was playing with Lego. He ignored her at first and they played side by side in silence for a while. Suddenly the child looked up.

Child	What are you making?
Adult	A house. Do you like it?
Child	Very small. I'm making a great big car.
Adult	I see. Where are its wheels?
Child	Hasn't got no wheels.
Adult	However will you get it to go without any wheels?
Child	Won't go. All the Lego wheels are lost.
Adult	I don't think they are. Have you looked in that box there?
Child	Oh, gosh! Lots of wheels here. Now my car'll go.

It was interesting to note that the classroom assistant did not interrupt the child's play when she first sat down at the table. Her activity caught the child's attention and a dialogue began. Although he asked a question about it, the little boy showed little interest in the adult's construction. She was aware of this, and took up his interest in the car that he was making. Later, the classroom assistant explained that this little boy engaged in a lot of solitary play of a constructive nature and that he was always prepared to accept situations just as they were. He would have left his car without wheels if the adult had not intervened!

Transcript 4 – In the painting area

In this area the additional teacher was having an individual conversation with the other hearing-impaired child about a picture that she had painted.

Teacher	What a beautiful pattern you've painted. I do like the colours.
Child	Red, blue, purple.
Teacher	Yes, you've used three colours – red, blue and purple.
Child	*(Pointing to the jars of paint)* Purple not there. I do it.
Teacher	*(Looking puzzled)* What did you do?
Child	*(Taking teacher's hand)* Come 'ere.
Teacher	Where are we going?
Child	Look. Red there, blue there, purple not there. I do purple.
Teacher	Oh, I see. You made the purple. There's no purple paint out there. How did you make it?
Child	Blue one, red one.
Teacher	I'd like to make some purple. What should I do?
Child	Blue one.
Teacher	*(Painting a blue square)* All right. I've put some blue on.
Child	Hurry up red one now.
Teacher	*(Painting a red square)* Now I've made a red square.
Child	Not like that. Put red one there.
Teacher	Oh, look! My blue is purple now too.
Child	That's right. Red one, blue one, purple one.
Teacher	I see. Red on top of blue makes purple.

The limited language of this six-year-old child illustrates just how ncecessary it is for an adult to become regularly involved in conversation with her. Through interactions of this nature she will learn how to put into words, that others will understand, the experiences that she is having. As the dialogue flowed along it was obvious that both adult and child were quite confident that they would be able to negotiate meaning. At this stage, for the little girl, this meant leading the teacher to the actual paint easel because she did not yet have sufficient language to deal with the situation verbally.

Conclusion

The atmosphere of the school into which a hearing-impaired child is placed is all important. If the child is to develop linguistically, he must feel that he is in a place where people share his interests and are anxious to discover what it is that he is trying to convey. The environment should be well planned, stimulating and one that provides opportunities for children to take the initiative.

If teachers can adopt a collaborative style which allows them to treat children as real partners in a conversation, at the early stages of the primary school, sound foundations will be laid, upon which more formal education can be built.

= 9 =
The Way Ahead

> *For those of us who are more knowledgeable and more mature – parents and teachers – the responsibility is clear; to interact with those in our care in such a way as to foster and enrich their meaning making.*
>
> (Wells, 1986)

No words could better sum up the role of parents and educators of hearing-impaired children. The responsibility is a joint one and this book has outlined ways in which parents and professionals can carry out their respective responsibilities, in partnership. This has been seen to involve following the stages of language development of children with normal hearing as closely as possible. Only in this way can hearing-impaired children have the opportunity to develop a degree of linguistic competence that gives them real access to normal society, thus forming a sound basis for the broadest possible education.

The book has concentrated on the early years of children with impaired hearing and it may, therefore, be helpful in conclusion to draw on the author's wider experience, so that projections may be made for the future of these young children who are enjoying an auditory oral way of life today. The author's experience has spanned the time in which hearing-aids have been developing and in which diagnostic and guidance services have been expanding. Conditions have been far from ideal during those years. However, even taking this factor into account, coming from a traditional 'oral' school background into an environment that has provided motivation for large numbers of severely and profoundly hearing-impaired children to develop normal, natural language through real life situations, it has been necessary, as each year has passed, to challenge previously held assumptions of what it is possible for these children to achieve. Expectations have risen year by year.

Where the management of the hearing loss is efficient, opportunities for hearing-impaired children have never before been as great as they are today. One of the most exciting features of the interactionist auditory oral approach is the large number of children for whom it is appropriate. The statistics from an analysis of the 1984–85 population of Birkdale School (Figures 1.1, 1.2, and 1.3) illustrate the wide range of children who can benefit from it.

Although the use of residual hearing is basic to the approach,

Figure 1.1 demonstrates that it is in use, not only with partially-hearing children, but also with those who have severe and profound hearing losses. If fitted with appropriate hearing-aids, each child is able to use to the full, whatever residual hearing he has. It is being found that children with very profound hearing losses are learning to listen and to make amazing use of minimal amounts of hearing. The proportion of children in Figure 1.1 with hearing losses over 100dB is high. As hearing-aids have improved, it has been necessary to raise expectations about the benefit that such children will gain from them. Hearing-impaired children receive the messages in a communication through a combination of listening and watching. The proportions in which they combine these vary greatly from child to child. It is interesting that these proportions are not determined wholly by the degree of hearing loss. The age at which the child was first issued with hearing-aids, the type of early listening environment in which the child had the opportunity to use them and the quality of interaction that he had within that environment, are all determining factors, as is the natural learning style of the child. It is sometimes forgotten that all children have their own individual learning styles. In any population of children with normal hearing, in a learning situation, some will depend heavily on visual cues, while for others the auditory cues will carry more information. It must always be remembered that hearing-impaired children display the same variety of basic characteristics as their hearing peers.

In Figure 1.2 there is evidence that not only bright children, but also those with average and below average ability, are to be found in an auditory programme. If the normal school population is considered, this should not really come as a surprise, because there is only a very small number of children with normal hearing who fail to develop fluency in their mother tongue. When the same type of language learning environment is created for hearing-impaired children, they too come through to a mastery of their mother tongue. This is usually in the same way as their hearing peers but at a slower rate. One clear indicator of this is to be found in the early attempts of children with significant hearing losses, in an interactionist auditory oral programme, to express themselves. Their early language often displays similar immaturities to those noted in the early language of children with normal hearing. A few examples taken from conversations held with six-year-olds with profound hearing losses (all 100dB or more across the speech range) illustrate this:

> 'He hitted me very hard.'
> 'I forget that, but I knowed it before.'
> 'First nobody at home – now all body there.'

These examples show hearing-impaired children trying to come to terms with the rules of their developing language and, in the early stages, applying these rules too generally because they have had too little experience to be aware of the irregularities.

In the author's experience it has been rather surprising to find that, quite often, the less able hearing-impaired children chatter more than those with more ability. This, too, has a parallel in children with normal hearing as the phrase 'empty vessels make most noise' bears out!

It is not only in the acquisition of language that hearing-impaired children, in truly auditory oral programmes, follow the developmental sequence of their hearing peers. An interesting longitudinal study, reported by Abberton *et al.* (1987) is producing results which indicate that in the areas of sound perception and speech production their progress follows the sequence of that of children with normal hearing, although development in these areas is undoubtedly delayed.

Figure 1.3 makes it abundantly clear that children from the lower social class groups are not exempted from an auditory oral programme. Indeed, over the years, the author has found that some of the parents who best seemed to understand and implement the principles of the approach were in the lower social class groups and, as with educational placement, the actual physical setting or group is not the vital factor. It is what happens between the hearing-impaired child and those within the setting, whatever that be, that determines what progress the child is likely to make.

Low educational attainment is widely reported in hearing-impaired children the world over. The figures in Conrad's (1979) study make depressing reading. It is a pity that these were not analysed to link specific results to specific backgrounds. Had this been done, the importance of the environment would have been highlighted. There is no doubt that low educational attainment is linked to the very limited linguistic competence of some hearing-impaired children. The interactionist auditory oral approach gives children experience across a wide range of linguistic functions and so, in classroom situations, they develop a flexibility of language that can form the basis for discussion in subjects, right across the curriculum. As a result, many come through to a level of educational attainment commensurate with their innate ability. The external examination results of the sixteen-year-olds in the Birkdale programme give some idea of what can be achieved by a completely unselected group of severely and profoundly hearing-impaired children, whose educational programme has been part of their auditory oral way of life. As these results are studied, it should be noted that most of the more able children in those years left Birkdale School at the age of eleven to take up a place in Mary Hare Grammar School for Hearing-Impaired Children. The results in Table 9.1, therefore, relate mainly to children with average and below average ability. A significant feature of the programme for these children, preparing for the Certificate of

Table 9.1 *Summary of examination results in Mode 1 Certificate of Secondary Education Examination (1976–85)*

Subject	Percentage of all leavers who sat examinations	Percentage of examination candidates who passed
Art, Design	96	99
English	68	80
Geometry & Engineering Drawing	44	89
Geography	68	85
History (only since 1981)	66	98
Home Economics	53	87
Mathematics	82	96
Needlework (only since 1979)	32	100
Science	69	99
Typewriting	41	83

Secondary Education examinations, was the proportion of time spent in oral discussion of the topics on the syllabus.

The author's recent experience in Turkey substantiates the claim that it is possible to implement this interactionist auditory oral approach in a completely different culture. The programme at Anadolou University, Eskişehir, is a completely new one and so its growth has been very rapid because it has not been hampered in any way by traditional thinking in relation to hearing-impaired children. A programme, based on the principles outlined in this book, has grown up to produce a population of chattering Turkish hearing-impaired children. Hearing-aids have been fitted to most of the children by the age of eighteen months and this is reflected in the pleasant quality of their voices. The parent guidance programme is helping parents to use the opportunities that normal daily life affords to establish communication with the hearing-impaired child. Emphasis has been placed on the quality of interaction between adult and child in the educational environment and timetables have been drawn up accordingly. At the same time, the programme has taken as its basis the syllabus followed in Turkish state schools for children with normal hearing. The two oldest groups of children, now at junior high school level, have developed sufficient competence in their mother tongue, Turkish, to be able to make a good start in learning English. There is no doubt that, in Turkey, as in Birkdale School and in other similar programmes, the forecast of Furness (1972) is proving correct:

> Everything points to a growing awareness that deaf children have the linguistic potential to achieve completely new standards of oralism, so bringing future generations to a higher level of educational achievement and a sense of belonging to the community at large.

It takes time for people to become aware of new possibilities and to implement change. The interactionist auditory oral approach is relatively new because it is less than twenty years since hearing-aids, which are powerful enough to meet the needs of children with profound hearing losses, have been freely available. Wherever it has been efficiently implemented, it has transformed the lives of many in a new generation of hearing-impaired young people. Those who have experienced the all-round advantages of a system that allows hearing-impaired children to learn language through living, in an environment planned to meet their special linguistic needs in a very normal way, are impatient to see more of today's children enjoying this way of life.

Groups of young hearing-impaired people all over the world have now developed fluent spoken language. The results are only gradually becoming known, because the approach is young in historical terms. However, as these results are collated from similar programmes worldwide, they cannot be ignored if professionals are to carry out their responsibilities to the present and future generations of hearing-impaired children.

References

ABBERTON, E., HAZAN, V. and FOURCIN, A. (1987) 'Speech pattern acquisition in profoundly hearing-impaired children' in *Proc. XIth Intnl. Congress of Phonetic Sciences USSR.*

BAMFORD, J. and SAUNDERS, S. (1985) *Hearing impairment, auditory perception and language ability.* London: Edward Arnold.

BESS, F. (1976) 'Condition of hearing-aids worn in a public school setting' in *The condition of hearing-aids worn by children (HEW publication 77-05002).* Washington, DC. US Bureau of Education for the Handicapped.

BRACKETT, D. and POLLACK, D. (1986) 'Auditory Learning', *Volta Review,* **88,** 5.

BRIAULT, E. (1982) 'The politics of contraction' in RICHARDS, C. (ed.) *New directions in Primary education.* Lewes: Falmer Press.

BRIERLEY, M. (ed.) (1969) *Fundamentals in the First School.* Oxford: Basil Blackwell.

BRITISH SOCIETY OF AUDIOLOGY (1988) 'Descriptors for Pure Tone Audiograms', *British Journal of Audiology,* **22,** 123.

BROWN, R. (1980) 'The maintenance of conversation' in OLSON, D. (ed.) *The social foundations of language and thought.* New York: Norton.

BRUCE, T. (1987) *Early childhood education.* London: Hodder and Stoughton.

BRUNER, J. (1983) *Child's Talk.* Oxford: Oxford University Press.

CLARK, M. (1985–86) *Developing the spoken language skills of hearing-impaired children.* 1 Laying the foundations (1985). 2 Building on the foundations (1986a). 3 Sounds all around (1986b). Manchester: MUTV, Manchester University.

CONRAD, R. (1979) *The deaf school child.* London: Harper and Row.

COOK, V.J. (1979) *Young Children and Language.* London: Edward Arnold.

CROWE, B. (1983) *Play is a feeling.* London: George Allen and Unwin.

CURTIS, A. (1986) *A curriculum for the pre-school child.* Windsor: NFER/Nelson.

DAVIES, B. (1981) 'Audiological and paediatric diagnosis and assessment' in MULLHOLLAND, A. (ed.) *Oral education today and tomorrow.* Washington: A.G. Bell Association.

DAWSON, F. (1977) 'Earmould production in vinyl – the end of feedback' in *J. Brit. Assn. Teachers of the Deaf,* **1,** 6.

DEPARTMENT OF EDUCATION AND SCIENCE (1981) *Education Act 1981: Special needs in education.* London: HMSO.

DE VILLIERS, P.A. and DE VILLIERS, J.G. (1979) *Early language.* London: Fontana.

DONALDSON, M. (1978) *Children's minds.* Glasgow: Fontana/Collins.

EDUCATION, SCIENCE AND ARTS COMMITTEE REPORT (1986) *Achievement in Primary schools.* London: HMSO.

EWING, I.R. and EWING A.W.G. (1954) *Speech and the deaf child.* Manchester: Manchester University Press.

FRY, D. and WHETNALL, E. (1954) 'The auditory approach in the training of deaf children', *Lancet,* **1,** 583–7.

FURNESS, H.J.S. (1972) 'The linguistic potential of deaf children', *Teacher of the deaf*, 70, 412.

GARVEY, C. (1984) *Children's Talk*. Oxford: Fontana.

HMI (1987) *Primary schools – some aspects of good practice*. London: HMSO.

HUIZING, H. (1960) 'Potential hearing in deaf children – its early development and use for auditory communication' in EWING, A. (ed.) *The Modern Educational Treatment of Deafness*. Manchester: Manchester University Press.

HUNTINGTON, A. (1986) *Sound experience through the radio hearing-aid* (video-tape). Manchester: MUTV, Manchester University.

HUNTINGTON, E. (1987) 'Personal experience of the impact of technology' in TAYLOR, I.G. (ed.) *The education of the deaf-current perspectives*, Vol. IV. London: Croom Helm.

KRETSCHMER, R. and KRETSCHMER, L. (1978) *Language development and intervention with the hearing impaired*. Baltimore: University Park Press.

LING, D. (1986) 'Devices and Procedures for Auditory Learning', *Volta Review*, 88, 5.

LING, D. and LING, A. (1978) *Aural Habilitation*. Washington: A.G. Bell Association.

LOCK, A. (1980) *The guided reinvention of language*. London: Academic Press.

LYNAS, W., HUNTINGTON, A. and TUCKER, I. (1988) *A critical examination of different approaches to communication in the education of deaf children*. Manchester: The Ewing Foundation.

MCMILLAN, M. (1919) *The Nursery School*. London: Dent.

MARKIDES, A. (1988) 'Speech Intelligibility: Auditory-Oral Approach versus Total Communication' *J. Brit. Assn. Teachers of the Deaf*, 12, 6.

MARTIN, A., BENTZEN, O., COLLEY, J., HENNEBART, D., HOLM, C., IURATO, S., DEJONGE, G., MCCULLEN, O., MEYER, M., MOORE, W. and MORGON, A. (1981) 'Childhood deafness in the European Community', *Scandinavian Audiology*, 10.

MEERS, H.J. (1976) *Helping our children talk*. London: Longman.

MINDEL, E.D. and VERNON, M. (1974) *They grow in silence*. Carlisle: British Deaf Association.

NOLAN, M. (1982) 'Modern developments in earmould technology – Implications for the profoundly deaf'. Paper presented at the XVIth International Congress of Audiology, Helsinki, Finland.

NOLAN, M. and TUCKER, I. (1981) *The hearing-impaired child and his family*. London: Souvenir Press.

OSBERGER, M.J. (ed.) (1985) *Language and learning skills of hearing-impaired students*. Omaha, NB: Boys Town Institute.

PATERSON, M.M. (1982) 'Integration of auditory training with speech and language for severely hearing-impaired children' in SIMS, D., WALTER, G. and WHITEHEAD, R. (eds) *Deafness and Communication*. Baltimore MD: Williams and Williams.

POLLACK, D. (1970) *Educational audiology for the limited hearing infant*. Springfield, Illinois: Charles Thomas.

PUGH, G. and DE'ATH, E. (1984) *The needs of parents*. London: Macmillan.

QUIGLEY, S.P. and KRETSCHMER, R.E. (1982) *The education of deaf children*. London: Edward Arnold.

REED, M. (1984) *Educating hearing-impaired children*. Milton Keynes: Open University Press.

ROSS, M. (1972) 'Classroom acoustics and speech intelligibility' in KATZ, J. (ed.) *Handbook of clinical audiology*. Baltimore: Williams and Williams.

STONE, P. and ADAM. A. (1986) 'Is your child wearing the right hearing-aid?', *Auditory Learning – Volta Review*, **88**, 5.

TAITE, M. (1986) 'Using singing to facilitate linguistic development in hearing-impaired pre-schools' in *J. Brit. Assn. Teachers of the Deaf*, **10**, 4, 103–8.

TAMBURRINI, J. (1982) 'New directions in nursery education' in RICHARDS, C. (ed.) *New directions in Primary education*. London: Falmer Press.

TIZARD, B. and HUGHES, M. (1984) *Young children learning*. London: Fontana.

TOUGH, J. (1977) *The development of meaning*. London: Allen and Unwin.

TUCKER, I. and NOLAN, M. (1984) *Educational Audiology*. London: Croom Helm.

TUCKER, I., HUGHES, M.E. and GLOVER, M. (1983) 'Verbal interaction with pre-school hearing-impaired children: a comparison of maternal and paternal language input' in *J. Brit. Assn. Teachers of the Deaf*, **7**, 4.

VAUGHAN, P. (1981) *Learning to listen*. Don Mills, Ontario: General Publishing Company.

WEBSTER, A. and ELLWOOD, J. (1985) *The hearing-impaired child in the ordinary school*. London: Croom Helm.

WELLS, G. (1981) *Learning through interaction*. Cambridge: Cambridge University Press.

WELLS, G. (1983) 'Talking with children: the complementary roles of parents and teachers' in DONALDSON, M., GRIEVE, R. and PRATT, C. (eds) *Early childhood development and education*. Oxford: Basil Blackwell.

WELLS, G. (1985) *Language development in the pre-school years*. Cambridge: Cambridge University Press.

WELLS, G. (1986) *The Meaning Makers*. London: Hodder and Stoughton.

WELLS, G. and NICHOLLS, J. (1985) *Language and learning: an interactional perspective*. London: Falmer Press.

WOOD, D. (1982) 'Fostering language development in hearing-impaired children' in CLARK, M. (ed.) *Special educational needs and children under five*. Educational Review Publications 9: University of Birmingham.

WOOD, D., MCMAHON, L. and CRANSTOUN, Y. (1980) *Working with under fives*. London: Grant McIntyre.

WOOD, D., WOOD, H., GRIFFITHS, A. and HOWARTH, I. (1986) *Teaching and talking with deaf children*. Chichester: John Wiley and Sons.

Index

accoustic feedback   22, 24, 63
amplification
  appropriate   18–20
  consistent   22, 33, 36
  limited   22
anxiety   8, 29–30, 41
attitudes
  of children   28
  of parents   27–8
  of professionals   25–6
auditory
  cues   10, 11, 14, 33, 36, 41, 84
  linguistic environment   11, 84
  way of life   7, 10–11, 15, 18, 19,
    22, 24, 60, 72, 76, 87

balance
  in interaction   49, 79
  in programmes   58, 60, 78

chatter   37, 42, 43, 47, 49, 65, 68
communication
  basis/foundation of   44, 47, 51,
    52, 56, 66
  competence/fluency in   15, 17,
    30, 32, 38, 41–2, 61, 72, 83
  oral/spoken   3, 6, 7–10, 11, 13,
    25, 72, 73, 75
  sign/manual   3, 7–9, 13–14, 15,
    35–6, 44, 62, 73–4
confidence   46, 67, 72, 78, 79, 82
conversation   11, 39, 45, 51, 66, 72,
    79, 82; see also interaction
conversational partner   36, 46, 48,
    68, 79, 82
counselling – see guidance

deaf   1, 3, 6, 7, 8, 9, 10, 15; see also
    hearing impaired
degrees of deafness   1–2
diagnosis   15, 16–18, 33, 38, 40, 41
dialogue   12, 77
  transcripts of   43, 45, 51, 52, 53,
    55, 81, 82

ear moulds   20–2, 63

Education Act (1981)   71–2
educational
  approaches   3–4
  attainment   75, 85–6
  placement   2–3, 58–60, 71–5
environment
  language learning   3–5, 11–12,
    37, 40–1, 47, 57, 73, 84
  listening   25, 26, 28–30, 32–3, 36
evidence   14–15
expectations   13–15, 41–2, 54, 61,
    83–4
experience
  of professionals   3, 13–14, 15
  shared   45, 66
eyes, as substitutes   9, 14, 33, 34–6

family   25, 26, 42, 48, 58, 61
fathers   46–7, 51–2

guidance, of parent   15, 25, 27, 30–
    2, 37, 40–2, 46, 48, 54–5, 86

hearing-aids
  benefits of   10, 19
  appropriate   18–20, 84
  maintenance/management   22–3,
    25, 33, 62
  review of   24
hearing age   40
hearing impairment/loss   1–2, 10,
    63
hearing potentials   5–6, 9–10, 11,
    14, 16, 20, 24, 28

interaction
  one-to-one   11, 15, 32, 38, 41,
    42–7, 48, 51, 54, 58, 61, 74, 75,
    79
  in play   30, 49, 67–8
integration   2, 15, 60, 73–4
initiative   53–4, 55, 82

linguistic competence – see
    communication
lipreading   3, 9–10, 34–5

listening/auditory awareness   3, 6,
     10, 14, 26–7, 28–32, 62, 84
listening conditions   34, 58

manual communication – *see*
     communication, signs/manual
mainstreaming – *see* integration
meaning
   shared/negotiated   10, 11, 36, 38,
     43, 45–6, 50, 51, 61, 68, 79, 83
mother/child routines   30, 39, 42–
     6, 78
motivation   11–12, 15, 35, 65, 83
music   54, 68–9, 78

noise   34, 58
nursery school – *see* pre-school

parents   6, 7–8, 13–15, 27–32, 56,
     64–5, 72–3, 85
   as partners   37, 40–2, 83
   as educators   44
perception, auditory – *see* sound
     perception
play
   adult intervention in   30, 49–50,
     67–8, 80–2
   creative   81–2
   exploratory   50
   importance of   49–50, 79
   imaginative/dramatic   52, 81
   materials   49, 53
   rule governed   52
   variety in   67
pre-school
   experience in   65–9
   language in   57–8, 66–8, 69

selection of   58–61
pre-school preparation
   of children   64
   of the hearing-impaired
     child   64–5
   of parents   64
   of staff   61–4
primary school
   age of entry   70–1
   language in   75–6, 77–9
   selection of/options   71–6
   transition to   76–7

rate of utterance   36
reading   55, 77
residual hearing – *see* hearing
     potential

silence/silent world   10, 18–19
sign language – *see* communication/
     sign
sound perception   85; *see also*
     listening/auditory awareness
special needs   2, 8, 58, 60, 62, 71–2,
     87
storytime   55, 68, 78

talk – *see* communication/oral
     conversation
teacher style   79–80
turn-taking   39
thinking   80

understanding – *see* meaning, shared

visual cues/vision   10, 11, 33, 34–5